1998
TOTAL HOROSCOPE
LIBRA
SEPT 23-OCT 22

JOVE BOOKS, NEW YORK

ASTROLOGICAL PERSPECTIVES BY MICHAEL LUTIN

THE PUBLISHERS REGRET THAT THEY CANNOT
ANSWER INDIVIDUAL LETTERS REQUESTING PERSONAL
HOROSCOPE INFORMATION

1996 TOTAL HOROSCOPE: LIBRA

PRINTING HISTORY
JOVE EDITION/JULY 1995

ISBN: 0-515-11667-X

A JOVE BOOK®
Jove Books are published by The Berkley Publishing Group,
200 Madison Avenue, New York, New York 10016.
JOVE and the "J" design
are trademarks belonging to Jove Publications, Inc.

PRINTED IN THE UNITED STATES OF AMERICA

CONTENTS

MESSAGE TO LIBRA

Dear Libra,
   Usually when you pick up a book on astrology, you turn to the Libra chapter and find out how sweet and gentle you are, how devoted and docile you're supposed to be, and what an utterly peaceful and harmonious life you lead. This is not the usual book. In the last five or six years many profound personal changes have taken place in you and, in fact, are still taking place. These changes will not truly be finished until the late 1980s.
   You have been feeling the effects of powerful planetary forces that have brought home a new sense of self. Many old relationships have ended, both personal and professional. New, healthier ones have taken their place: where you once could bend completely to the wishes of others, you have now tried to assert yourself on your own, to make some decisions and lead a life of freedom and adventure without vacillation, indecision, or the old preoccupation with "being alone or not being alone." It has been a time of important additions and removals, sudden reversals, separations, losses, scandals or last-minute changes of plans, and especially events. Your energy level has been high; you have a love for excitement, risk and adventure. You've become involved with unusual kinds of relationships based on new feelings of independence, freedom and equality. In a sense, you've become liberated. You've learned a tremendous amount about yourself, what you are, what you need. You've been searching for a sense of who you are, apart from your desires to please others and to satis-

5

fy the wishes of those around you. Well, who are you, after all?

You, of all the signs in the Zodiac, profit the most from companionship. You are relationship-oriented, although this does not necessarily refer to marriage. You have a warm, friendly personality that is often geared toward attracting and pleasing others. When you are making contact, you are affable and loving. You can really enjoy the feeling of striking up a kinship or connecting with another human being. You often seek to unite with others on a mental, sexual, emotional or business level. Ideally you are a joiner, with a true desire to find another human being with whom to share your joys.

You are generous and considerate, but when you feel you are extending yourself too much without enough in return, or when you feel people are taking advantage of you, you are resentful. Although you may resent the role you play, in the past you have hidden your hostilities. You have not wanted to admit there was anything wrong, and as a result you have taken a defensive, submissive stand in an effort to keep peace. By concealing your discontent, you may have taken on unnecessary pain and put yourself in an unfortunate position. You may even have jeopardized a whole relationship by not speaking up about what was bothering you. Instead of voicing your views, bringing problems out in the open, and confronting serious issues head-on, you may have remained silent until the breaking point. Then an explosion may have been necessary to awake everybody to the fact that things were out of whack.

You're a kind person at heart, with the ability of a great leader to recognize other people's needs, foibles, and strategies. Your heart is noble and your motives are often well-disposed and considerate. You have a natural gift of diplomacy and are greatly skilled at the bargaining table. What is needed is the development of that skill. If you fail to exercise your capacity in bringing out the truth, or if you even fear trying, you will often fall into a bitter, resentful silence. You will not only be failing your partner by robbing him of your diplomatic skill in problem-solving, but you will be turning the anger inward on yourself. Such feelings can result in illness, upset, or violent outburst.

You have the capacity for delicacy of taste, refinement and artistry. Contrary to what most people think, there *are* Libras with vulgar, crude tastes and sensibilities. They are often defensive and insecure, covering their obstinacy and selfishness and fear of people with a gentle smile. As a rule, though, you have a fine sense of harmony and grace, and you were born with an appreciation for the beautiful. No matter what forces you constantly come up against, you are striving for peace and unity. Only in the last few years have you been able to confront many problems openly. You have always tried to restore balance and maintain a steady, even keel. Sometimes you have even upset the balance yourself, just to see how quickly you could regain equilibrium.

You can be the spirit of companionship personified. You have sometimes been too hasty in your desire to latch on to someone. You can propose one minute and run away the next. You can often be too interested in being available and involved in courtship and the chase, to get down to seriously relating to anyone. But when you feel warmth from another person, if it strikes you right, you are joyous and helpful, warm, affectionate and giving, conciliatory and willing to compromise. You can be a faithful mate. You look to your spouse for light, traditional in the sense that you believe in old values about people needing each other and being together.

Yours is the sign of partnership, after all, and partnership is equality. You are providing something for your mate that is your unique and special gift. Your spouse has other qualities that you need. This is the basis of all partnerships. You can fall in love with someone and marry. Then you can discover countless little things that annoy or disturb you. Although you are openly easygoing, there is a hidden perfectionist streak in you that is constantly criticizing your partner. Unless you understand yourself—what your needs are, what you're like when it comes to signing on the dotted line, relationships—you will be disillusioned and discontented in marriage.

If you find yourself repeating similar mistakes, being attracted to the same kinds of people who do not ultimately bring you happiness, then you have to go back and review your whole situation. Often you will marry first and ask questions afterward, since one of your best ways to find out about yourself has always been to find somebody else to relate to. While this is romantic and often leads to a fulfilling, happy, life-long marriage, sometimes it does not.

You really ought to determine what it is you want in a human being, and then go out and look for it. Many people have complicated backgrounds and confusing emotional lives. Others have desires or priorities that make it difficult to fulfill themselves when it comes to marriage. It *is* possible for everyone to find another human being with whom he can be happy. First, though, you have to be willing to be happy. You have to *want* to give of yourself to another. You have to *want* to share ups and downs, joys and sorrows, and face sides of yourself that may annoy and frustrate you. You have to *want* to share facets of your personality which you have always kept to yourself.

But life is growth, and growth is the mutual sharing of life's benefits, trials, surprises and blessings. You have to seek out the truth, find out exactly what it is that makes you happy and whole, what fulfills you and completes you as a human being. Much of life is based on relationships, whether we enjoy the idea or not. You need to radiate love and warmth, and you need to find it outside and receive it yourself. Trade is necessary, for it reflects your ability to grasp another's reality and relate it to your own. To do that successfully takes love, tact, consideration and loads of understanding.

Some of your basic needs are to understand and fulfill the needs of your mate. You may rebel, fight for independence and demand equal time, but you have to know what to demand when you finally get a hearing. Unless your bid for independence was an empty rebellion, unless your belief in personal liberty and truth has been in vain, unless the strange upheaval of the past years has served no purpose, you must now know what you want in any partnership or relationship, and you should have learned how to ask for it.

You are on the prowl constantly, demurely considering seduction and turning shyly away from admirers. You can sit and smile with saccharine insincerity while inwardly criticizing or making plans for your getaway. You act dependent and meek, and often like to lean on a strong shoulder. You are too quick to surrender authority or responsibility, but you resent it if you are not considered a leader. Why then do Libras make great generals? Generals are masters of strategy. They are constantly thinking of the other guy's move. They anticipate his needs and reactions. They know how to be at the right place at the right time because they have become skilled at thinking through the mind of their adversary. Although generals exercise generous and just command over their troops and lead them on to victory, they do not necessarily make good presidents. A Libra who is in the Number One position and is good at it has developed diplomacy to the fullest.

You want somebody around most of the time, and you are really good at extending yourself to make sure someone else is okay and happy. But you get tired of it. When you start saying you think you need some time off to yourself, it's the perfect moment to inject a little romance into the situation. You are trying to get away from limitation and routine. You need to feel pursued, wanted, sought after, desirable. If your situation becomes too ordinary or humdrum you feel safe, but discontented. You need to be wooed. Actually, wooing is more your preference than anyone else's. You are often attracted to free, independent, thoughtless or selfish types. Lately that may have changed. The shoe may have recently been on the other foot. But in general, you are often more conscious of getting together, marrying and so on than the people you are attracted to. You are the marrying kind. Whether you like the idea or not, it's true. You are conscious of relationships and have to relate to something. You must have a person, place or thing in your life that is drawing most of your attention while at the same time sustaining you. You always have some major someone or some major something that you are relating to and trying to win over in some way.

You can seem concerned and sincere when actually you are not. You can sound as though you're giving in when you're actually plotting to get your own way. You can cloak your selfishness in a mantle of tactful rationalization. You may have no interest in going further than ingratiating superficiality in a half-baked effort to meet the "peson of your dreams." As a writer, composer or actor you can be magnificent. Your successes come from your sense of ideal beauty, plus a capacity to look through the eyes of the rest of the world. You are conservative most of the time, but the past few years have shown you a great departure from your usual conduct and point of view, presenting you with lifestyles you would have thought scandalous before. Still, you have a streak of reserve that comes from your desire to offend nobody and please everybody. Although events and behavior have certainly been extreme over the past few years, you are not an extremist and do not enjoy the extremist sides of your personality. As soon as a definite extreme is visible, you hasten to find enough of the opposite trait to balance it out.

You like to think that you have gifts and talents, originality and independence, but you often abhor the extremist behavior and high risk associated with such temperaments. It has only been recently that new sides of your character have suddenly come to the surface. Experience has taught you the value and consequence of upsetting a scene that may have lacked a lot of things but certainly had equilibrium. It is necessary to take risks in the hope of discovering new ways to be happy. It is important to liberate yourself from fears and frustrations. But when unexpected events occur, you have to know how to react spontaneously without looking to anyone for advice—*if* you really want to be independent. You are certainly noticing the changes going on within yourself.

What you can find as a Libra is your true relationship. Compatibility is harmony, yes. It is also the equilibrium reached by two different people with two different sets of ideas and values, living and working in the same environment. If you've won anything in the battle for freedom, justice and equality, let it be a step in your development as a loving, desirable partner. It is too easy to be carried away by illusions of newfound power. Separations and unexpected reversals can cause rifts that are impossible to heal. Open yourself up to new experience and prepare for a new honesty that will create a new you.

Relationships are many things for many people. If you try to be everybody's ideal, you'll never have a clear picture of what you want and need. You'll never be sure exactly who should be the one to love you.

Love is a fantastic thing—it is the feeling of knowing that someone else's life is better just because you're in it. No matter what hardships arise or personal struggles go on, you're there together to share and sustain each other. We all need to know someone is there to care about us. It is our way of relating to eternity. We all need confrontation, opposition, healthy competition and a field on which to play out our emotional drama.

Relationships fall apart mainly because both people

have given up. When one of the partners stops working at the relationship, there's still a chance to keep it alive. All people go through personal crises. At one time or another *you* may get weary and bored, or perhaps your spouse may lose interest. It's natural and it happens in every relationship. But as long as one of you is still concerned, there's still a chance.

You need companionship, something to live for. Without it you often feel you have nothing to live for. With it you often feel you have no life of your own. You are searching to find a balance between lonely separatism and unwholesome dependence. It's certain that your sense of self will grow as you develop the capacity to share.

Michael Lutin

A SNEAK PREVIEW
OF THE LATE '90s

As the last decade of the twentieth century comes to a close, planetary aspects for its final years connect you with the future. Major changes completed in 1995 and 1996 form the bridge to the twenty-first century and new horizons. The years 1997 through 1999 and into the year 2000 reveal hidden paths and personal hints for achieving your potential, your message from the planets.

Libra individuals, ruled by Venus, the planet of love and beauty, are buoyed by expectations of the good life. The key is Pluto in Sagittarius from late 1995 to the year 2007. Pluto, the planet of transformation, affects Libra communications. The good-luck planet Jupiter, which rules Sagittarius, has positive vibrations with Venus, also considered a planet of good fortune.

Libra optimism is accentuated by Sagittarius, sign of expansiveness and enthusiasm. Travel and exploration, studies and higher education are emphasized. You can achieve balance and harmony through learning about yourself and the people close to you. You must avoid restlessness, waste, lavish spending. The opportunities for the good life are there as long as you take advantage of the good luck brought by Jupiter and Venus.

A growing sense of self and responsibility coming from Saturn, which rules Capricorn and Aquarius, protects you from reckless action, risks, and fanciful thinking. Capricorn, like Libra, is a cardinal sign, so expect great activity and stress. Contradiction and crisis can be turned to your advantage as you exercise the tact and diplomacy for which you are famous. Jupiter in Capricorn 1996 and early 1997 frees you from indecisiveness and helps you persevere. With patient effort you reap the rewards of love and money. Jupiter in Aquarius 1997 to early 1998 sharpens your social and intellectual skills, making you highly productive and eager to innovate. Long periods of study and application can bring your goals to fruition.

Saturn is in Aries from April 1996 to March 1999. Aries is your zodiacal partner as well as your zodiacal opposite. Pioneering Aries leads you on a search for new connections. While travel and exploration broaden your horizons, you never lose sight of your primary urge to connect with people. Jupiter in Aries early 1999 to spring 2000 continues the trend of exploration on the frontier. Saturn enters Taurus March 1999. Libra has a tie to Taurus by sharing Venus as a ruling planet. With Saturn in Taurus into the year 2002, you have no qualms about hazarding the frontier and encountering its inevitable risks.

Aquarius, an air sign like yours, further emphasizes movement and freedom as the century turns. Aquarius strikes a note of impersonality in Libra relationships. Love partners blend into your work life and social life. The stakes of partnerships and alliances are waged more for intellectual gain and material opportunity than mere pleasure or vanity.

Uranus, planet of independence and the unexpected, is in Aquarius January 1996 to the year 2003. Uranus in Aquarius bridges the creative impulse and the intellectual imperative, so you balance private life with public life and community service. The idealism of Sagittarius fires the intellect of Aquarius, while sober Saturn judges the risks. Neptune, planet of vision as well as illusion, is in Capricorn until late November 1998. Neptune in Capricorn gives determination to Libra creative energy and stabilizes your airy temperament. Neptune is in Aquarius 1998 to the year 2011. Neptune in Aquarius blows the winds of good fortune over your artistic life, allowing your visions to flourish.

NOTE TO THE CUSP-BORN

Are you *really* a Libra? If your birthday falls around the fourth week in September, at the very beginning of Libra, will you still retain the traits of Virgo, the sign of the Zodiac before Libra? What if you were born late in October—are you more Scorpio than Libra? Many people born at the edge, or cusp, of a sign have great difficulty in determining exactly what sign they are. If you are one of these people, here's how you can figure it out, once and for all.

Consult the table on page 17. It will tell you the precise days on which the Sun entered and left your sign for the year of your birth. If you were born at the beginning or end of Libra, yours is a lifetime reflecting a process of subtle transformation. Your life on Earth will symbolize a significant change in consciousness, for you are either about to enter a whole new way of living or are leaving one behind.

If you were born at the beginning of Libra, you may want to read the horoscope book for Virgo as well as Libra, for Virgo holds the keys to much of the complexity of your spirit, reflects certain hidden weaknesses, uncertainties, and your secret wishes. You are eager to get involved with another person, yet you are often pulled back from total involvement by your sense of propriety or your wish to be pure and unspoiled. You hover between poetic romanticism and stiff mental analyzation. At best, your powers of criticism serve you to develop your potentials and enhance the life of your partner. In that way, you are helpful and loving, considerate and faithful—a pure marriage of mind and body, head and heart.

If you were born at the end of Libra you may want to read the horoscope book for Scorpio as well as Libra. Scorpio dominates your finances, money, assets, potentials and your values in general. While your sexual expectancies can be naive, unrealistic and adolescent, you are passionate, excitable and highly seductive.

You may vacillate between a desire to please another and a fanatical determination to maintain control and survive on your own. You can love with a fatal obsession, where you will blind your eyes to keep peace in a relationship—then suddenly declare war. Although you could prolong the agony of a situation in order to avoid a confrontation, you are the personification of awakening passion and a spirit that longs for the joys of companionship and the simple harmonies of life.

DATES SUN ENTERS LIBRA
(LEAVES VIRGO)

September 23 every year from 1900 to 2000, except for the
following:

	September 22:			September 24:
1948	1968	1981	1992	1903
52	72	84	93	07
56	76	85	96	
60	77	88	97	
64	80	89		

DATES SUN LEAVES LIBRA
(ENTERS SCORPIO)

October 23 every year from 1900 to 2000, except for the
following:

October 22:	October 24:			
1992	1902	1911	1923	1943
96	03	14	27	47
	06	15	31	51
	07	18	35	55
	10	19	39	59

LOVE AND RELATIONSHIPS

No matter who you are, what you do in life, or where your planets are positioned, you still need to be loved, and to feel love for other human beings. Human relationships are founded on many things: infatuation, passion, sex, guilt, friendship, and a variety of other complex motivations, frequently called love.

Relationships often start out full of hope and joy, the participants sure of themselves and sure of each other's love, and then end up more like a pair of gladiators than lovers. When we are disillusioned, bitter, and wounded, we tend to blame the other person for difficulties that were actually present long before we ever met. Without seeing clearly into our own natures we will be quite likely to repeat our mistakes the next time love comes our way.

Enter Astrology.

It is not always easy to accept, but knowledge of ourselves can improve our chances for personal happiness. It is not just by predicting when some loving person will walk into our lives, but by helping us come to grips with our failures and reinforce our successes.

Astrology won't solve all our problems. The escapist will ultimately have to come to terms with the real world around him. The hard-bitten materialist will eventually acknowledge the eternal rhythms of the infinite beyond which he can see or hear. Astrology does not merely explain away emotion. It helps us unify the head with the heart so that we can become whole individuals. It helps us define what it is we are searching for, so we can recognize it when we find it.

Major planets have been operating on the sign of Libra and have changed people's ideas about love and commitment. Since Libra is the sign of marriage, partnerships, and relationships, these factors have affected virtually everyone in areas of personal involvement. These forces point out upheavals and transformations occurring in all of society. The concept of marriage is being totally reexamined. Exactly what the changes will ultimately bring no one can tell. It is usually difficult to determine which direction society will take. One thing is certain: no man is an island. If the rituals and pomp of wedding ceremonies must be revised, then it will happen.

Social rules are being revised. Old outworn institutions are indeed crumbling. But relationships will not die. People are putting less stress on permanence and false feelings of security. The emphasis now shifts toward the union of two loving souls. Honesty, equality, and mutual cooperation are the goals in modern marriage. When these begin to break down, the marriage is in jeopardy. Surely there must be a balance between selfish separatism and prematurely giving up.

There is no doubt that Astrology can establish the degree of compatibility between two human beings. Two people can share a common horizon in life but have quite different habits or basic interests. Two others might have many basic characteristics in common while needing to approach their goals from vastly dissimilar points of view. Astrology describes compatibility based on these assumptions.

It compares and contrasts through the fundamental characteristics that draw two people together. Although they could be at odds on many basic levels, two people could find themselves drawn together again and again. Sometimes it seems that we keep being attracted to the same type of individuals. We might ask ourselves if we have learned anything form our past mistakes.

The answer is that there are qualities in people that we require and thus seek out time and time again. To solve that mystery in ourselves is to solve much of the dilemma of love, and help ourselves determine if we are approaching a wholesome situation or a potentially destructive one.

We are living in a very curious age with respect to marriage and relationships. We can easily observe the shifting social attitudes concerning the whole institution of marriage. People are seeking everywhere for answers to their own inner needs. In truth, all astrological combinations can achieve compatibility. But many relationships seem doomed before they get off the ground. Astrologically there can be too great a difference between the goals, aspirations, and personal outlook of the people involved. Analysis of both horoscopes must and will indicate enough major planetary factors to keep the two individuals together. Call it what you will: determination, patience, understanding, love—whatever it may be, two people have the capacity to achieve a state of fulfillment together. We all have different needs and desires. When it comes to choosing a mate, you really have to know yourself. If you know the truth about what you are really looking for, it will make it easier to find. Astrology is a useful, almost essential, tool to that end.

YOU AND YOUR MATE

LIBRA—ARIES

You have both been under heavy stress since way back in 1970. Unexpected reversals, changes, and removals have characterized your lives, and partnerships have taken unusual turns. It's a question of independence, really, and reflects basic questions between people, their commitments, their ability to form lasting unions and their desire to cooperate with each other. Role-playing in sexual and emotional relationships is the key here.

Active or passive, aggressive or shy, independent or dependent, you have both learned how to cope with disruption, separation, and strange reversals. You have both learned how important it is to have a life separate from the relationship in order to avoid exhausting the resources of the relationship. You are still seeking to find your true self—the "you" defined by nobody but yourself, on your own terms, for better or worse, like it or not. If you wrap yourself up totally in your mate, defer constantly to your partner, and plan all your life around one person, you may resent it and lose your self-esteem and confidence. Yet to destroy a good relationship can take away one of your major joys in living. Aim to blend self-fulfillment with the capacity to cooperate to the greatest degree.

Independence, equality and awareness must characterize a long-range period of change and growth.

Hints for Your Aries Mate:

In this relationship you have one tough cookie on your hands. Try not to depend too much on the notion that opposites attract, and search deeply for what you two have in common. You may get Aries to go along with your passion for joint projects, if you are willing to give more support than leadership. Your mate is likely to balk if she or he is not allowed a free and independent hand. This partnership may spend your diplomacy and talents for smoothing over. If you truly want to make a go of it, let your mate go off on his or her own. That way you will preserve your identity, which Aries often tries to envelop. Show off your elegant and sophisticated sides. Aries will gobble up anything you have to say about style whether it be in art or high couture. She or he will be proud of your good taste and sexually attracted to your refined sensibilities.

LIBRA—TAURUS

As you went through a long period of turbulence a couple of years ago, now Taurus is feeling the effects of reversals, abrupt changes, high energy levels. What has come over that calm disposition? Taurus has been experiencing the need for space, change, and excitement. You can understand what Taurus is going through, for you have felt the same way. You can appreciate the upheavals, sudden drastic decisions, changes and irrepressible restlessness.

You are both born under the planet Venus and are thus drawn together by your shared love of beauty, pleasure and fulfillment. Together, you are a blend of rugged, raw material and refined artistic sensibilities. You both love the luxuries and all the blessings of this life. When you feel threatened by each other, you can get mighty competitive, materialistic, almost crude. Your

Taurus can be a great asset, of course, both materially and emotionally, but when problems of sex and money make it hard for you to relate healthily, you can feel that Taurus is your sole liability. At worst, you are a pair of indecisive status-seekers, afraid to make any changes and upset an already stagnant equilibrium.

At best, you are a gracious and charming couple, united in your love of beauty and need for loyalty, security and feeling. You have a gift for charity, elegance and comfort that warms people, puts them at ease and makes them pleased to be in your company.

Hints for Your Taurus Mate:

Pay a lot of sexual attention to Taurus if you expect to be the apple of your partner's eye. Your mutual penchant for beautiful goods could lead to the poorhouse—for you, but not for Taurus who has a cache of money in the basement of a pokey little bank you've never heard of. Taurus is essentially proud of his or her frugal ways, and will expect praise for finding a bargain no matter how trivial. You'll cotton to your mate's refusal to be rushed in decision making. But you'll cringe when you can make a quick emotional connection while your partner develops a dense look in the eyes. Consider Taurus' density as a restraint on your impetuosity, and you won't slip into contempt. Contrive ways to keep stick-in-the-mud Taurus out of the house. Meet directly after work for drinks or dig up a sale on the other side of town. Once you are out, Taurus sparkles and bubbles.

LIBRA—GEMINI

You are a couple who needs people. You're lucky because you combine gentleness of spirit with boldness of mind. You blend tact, diplomacy and the subtlety of personal attraction with the capacity of knowing how to talk to people on different levels. You can share love on verbal or nonverbal levels, for you bring each other a passive harmony and artistic sensibility joined to the curious quality of a hungry intellect. Although your relationship could lose its glow quickly and make you tire of each other, you can send each other higher and higher with an exciting combination of shy seductiveness and bold experimentalism. It could be a wearisome relationship of vacillation and flirtation, weekend trysts and superficial attachments, but it's really a novel romance, as lovely as a trip to Paris in June.

As a pair, you need changes of scene, constant amusement and renewed interests. Instead of merely collecting people like notches on a gun, your need is to go outside the relationship in order to meet people, and thus renew the resources of your relationship. It may be that your relationship is richest in a mental, philosophical sense, bringing you closer to your true codes of ethics and religious beliefs. The light, airy quality you share makes yours a harmonious match of wills.

Hints for Your Gemini Mate:

The danger of this mating lies in the superficial side of your natures. Gemini will adore your social and partying ways and expect you to maintain them. You needn't be afraid of competition when you flash your wit and charm. Gemini will consider your verbal abilities a homage to those same qualities in him or her. But you will be expected to keep up the performance to hold Gemini's interest. Turn to your work to hide your depression. Work is about the only competitor that your mate respects. Avoid mention of emotional pain, or your mate's exit will be swift. A few words of praise, however, will bring out the warm and nurturing side of Gemini. Then you will be the recipient of innumerable bowls of chicken soup or cups of tea to lift you from the dumps.

With a little help from your friends, family, and the neighbors, you'll survive the relationship.

LIBRA—CANCER

You are both devoted to the ideas of marriage and family, partnerships and security, both personally and in business. Your combined efforts can bring them home and make them come true. You are both shrewd and know how to bend to get your way. You know how to yield, retreat, feel each other out and use all your powers of tact, strategy and intuition to keep the roof over your heads and the wolf from the door.

Vacillating and withdrawn, you could each shut your eyes to facts, smile and go on clinging to the decks of a sinking ship—just digging deeper into an unrealistic world of false security and safety. During the past few years, you have both undergone tremendous upheavals, reversals, removals, changes and unexpected additions that have put your lives on a new course. Long-range changes are slow in coming, but they are long-lasting.

You both need love, warmth and the tenderness found in a deep relationship. You both need to accept your own selfishness and coolness, to develop a sense of who you are that is defined by the facts of your lives. You need to go on pouring your love outward, and not worry about what you are getting back. Successful union is based on mutual cooperation, acceptance and victory over the limitations our life situations try to impose. Share your lives.

Hints for Your Cancer Mate:

Your needs are your Cancer lover's needs. Work toward a healthy and long-lasting relationship by opening up your domestic life. Invite friends and acquaintances to share your meals and company as often as you can afford. Cancer needs all the coaxing and encouragement he or she can get in order to come out from under his or her rock. Try to restrain your jolly-them-out-of-it side, or you will have a constantly tearful lover on your hands. If you love your Moon Child, don't let Cancer fade into the woodwork and especially not into you. Be sure you exercise your powers of bringing out the best in others, and your mate will bloom. Cancer is a real wiz when it comes to repairing household gadgets or creating exotic meals. Buy your partner unusual cookbooks and a box of tools to encourage experimentation in the home. To get lots of affection, give lots.

LIBRA—LEO

You've got the possibility of a warm, loving and responsive relationship. Together you can share love and affection, companionship, security and financial success. You are both friendly, harmonious people deep down and can be considerate as well as passionate. It's a comfortable connection, at times as close and easy as brother and sister.

You've got to contend with an ego that can be revoltingly insatiable and controlling, or a harmlessness that can take the joy and fire out of living. You may get bored and restless. At worst, your relationship can degenerate into meaningless noncommunication that will skirt basic issues and problems. It can be a contest of arrogance and vanity, pomp and flattery, where you spend half your time puffing up an ego, the other half knocking it down.

At best, you are true companions. If at times you are a little detached, you are still friendly. You can be the perfect combination for love and marriage. You are the blend of stability and mutual support, the union of strength and weakness. As a pair you will be most successful when you change rude selfishness into stable,

life-giving love, and chaotic, panicked dependency into
sincere consideration for your mate.

Hints for Your Leo Mate:

With this relationship you won't have to hold back on
love. Leo will take all you have to offer and more. Your
mate will not tolerate pressure, so ease off on your urge
to squeeze. And don't sulk when you find her or him
outdoing you in every area. Leo has nothing but contempt for those who won't turn competition into a
creative outlet. Your mate's energy and leadership will
force you out of your bed of depression and into the
arena. The black-or-white view may cause you to bite
your tongue, but it will also give you a chance to practice your belief in live and let live. Leo's desire to win at
everything is only a desire to attract you sexually. Buy
your mate a membership in a tennis club or a health spa;
permit a lot of bragging about outshining everybody in
the club or spa. Letting your partner beat her or his
breast is the way to win Leo's heart.

LIBRA—VIRGO

Virgo is the source of Libra's spiritual unfolding and
will awaken your sense of renunciation, sacrifice, compassion and cosmic mystery. Both of you crave the companionship and the bond of love and sharing, but may
be pulled back from total commitment, mentally and
physically, by guilt, a sense of propriety or a secret wish
to be pure and unspoiled. Together you blend a
monastic simplicity with gracious beauty, a marriage of
mind and body.

As a pair you can be indecisive and nervous, even
downright emotionally dishonest. Too much passivity
or shyness will keep this relationship from blossoming.
What you need is a little zest, some zip and passion to

enhance the quiet friendliness of your association. You need some healthy confrontations to keep from going mad from politeness. Neither of you will enjoy causing trouble and making waves, for you are peaceful souls seeking happiness in each other's company. You will stimulate Virgo's money-making capacity in some way and will yourself be drawn to Virgo for partnership, companionship, advice and love. You may flee from Virgo, only to return and renew time and again.

Forgiveness and trust open the way for you spiritually where Virgo is concerned. Then disillusion can become love, confusion can become love, and guilt can become love. Work is the secret key.

Hints for Your Virgo Mate:

Play your cards openly in this relationship and you will be touched more deeply than you ever have been. Don't fight Virgo's healing power, or your mate will withdraw it for good. If you don't kick and scream, Virgo will open spiritual doors for you. When you feel a fit coming on, take to the sidewalks and walk it off. You'll return refreshed and ready for your mate's soothing hand. With Virgo, trust in reacting instead of acting. Let your mate fascinate but not hypnotize you. With your elegant taste it will be a cinch to appeal to the esthetic in her or him. Just when you think you are both hopelessly spaced out, Virgo will jolt you into action. What your partner needs is your patience in lovemaking. Arrange a romantic night for two at least once a month. At a secluded dinner by candlelight, woo your mate with wine and song. Then wait for the fireworks.

LIBRA—LIBRA

Together you mean marriage. When you two form a partnership, you do everything possible to keep it alive.

You are tactful and diplomatic, careful and considerate. You know how to go after what you want by taking your partner along. You know how to bend, expand or contract when necessary, alter your plans, develop your strategies and share your experiences, all to keep things steady, for your concern for your partner's well-being is genuine. When you find something you want outside the relationship, you will resort to deception to avoid sharing it or an open confrontation that will make you take decisive action or force you into irrevocable choices. You will see yourselves in terms of each other.

At worst, you will waver and wiggle, and never dare fulfill yourselves. You will spend your days on a seesaw, bouncing around and trying to get your partner to suggest what you want to do yourself.

At best, you are the unified spirit of cooperation, justice and understanding. You will set about to implement long-range changes in your individual personalities. Ideas of marriage, partnership and relationship are going through great changes, and they will reflect your deeper sense of yourselves separately and together for a long time to come.

Hints for Your Libra Mate:

What you are up against is a mirror image. You can be certain that your Libra won't step on your romantic toes. The problem will be to cut through the grace and essential politeness of this union. Your best bet is a catalyst. Seek out friends who will not kowtow to you and your Libra mate's need for fantasy. If you can't find an abrasive friend, join a primal therapy group for as long as you can stand it. Think of yourself as a performer who has to cut through the murky, otherworldly environment of an abstract play. Take on the role of guiding the two of you through the mist and fog. Ground yourself by partaking in sports, repulsive as that may seem to both of you. Get up early and jog around the park. Follow with a cold shower and a lively political discussion over breakfast. If you both still have energy, trust that love will see you through.

LIBRA—SCORPIO

One powerful Scorpio effect on you will be financial. Your material condition will change slowly but permanently. Deep within you, greed will either wake up or die, for over a long peiod of time you will be developing a whole new sense of values. You will learn to survive.

You may fall into an almost obsessive relationship with Scorpio. You may feel you are being irresistibly drawn closer and closer to a power you find fascinating, hypnotic, magic. Because of it your life will change slowly, bringing a permanent revision of everything you hold dear. You may sense a connection between you that is inexorable, inevitable, one that can never be severed.

You will need clever tactics and skillful manipulation for this one, for your relationship plays and dances between a desire to please others and a fanatical determination to maintain control. Yours is a delicate balance between peace and war. Together you mark the point of turning on to the passions and ecstatic bliss of llfe. You personify the awakening of desire.

The passage of the planet Pluto through Libra during the next few years brings you closer to Scorpio than ever, for Pluto is the planetary ruler of Scorpio. Here are planted the seeds of change in your relationship, tending either toward destruction and turmoil, or toward total spiritual enlightenment.

Hints for Your Scorpio Mate:

The daring, dangerous sides of your nature will come to the surface in a relationship with Scorpio. You'll have to fight to maintain your view from both sides of the fence.

Your fear of being sucked up in the whirlwind created by your mate should not prevent you from seeing that your mate fears your powers of amelioration. Deep and deadly game-playing could be the result of your combined terrors. It will be up to you to nip these emotional jousts in the bud; act out your terrors with harmless games. Pit yourself against your mate in checkers, chess, or monopoly. If board games become too tame, get your mate to join a softball or volleyball team. To make the game interesting, join an opposing team and bring your partner's dark forces out into the open where you have an even chance. Don't pull your punches, and the relationship may endure.

LIBRA—SAGITTARIUS

Your friendship should be full of grace and good cheer, consideration and enthusiasm. You will always try to be gracious hosts and project a happy image to the world, no matter what's going on in private.

Although you can both lack discipline and decisiveness, your interests are many and your approach positive. Both of you may have difficulty mastering your skills, and you should avoid glossing over deep problems until they are staring you in the face. Yet you are both truth seekers and defenders of justice. You love to be happy and enjoy life, and you need pleasant surroundings. Art, beauty and the pleasures of a friendly relationship should be the main purpose of your lives, for your greatest achievements will come through selfless sharing.

When you allow yourselves to be lawless and sloppy, self-indulgent and immature, you will let life carry you along deeper and deeper into serious unpleasant consequences. When you fail to confront difficulties and continue to bury them, time will force them to the surface. As you deal with realities when they come up, your relationship will deepen into a mutually supportive one.

Together you reflect a need for permanence and marital stability plus the desire to be free, uncommitted and eternally available for any possibility that happens your way. Try to develop maturity, patience and a sense of reality.

Hints for Your Sagittarius Mate:

With a Sagittarius lover you can cash in on your gracious-living image. There will be no need to hide your passion for the good things in life. Your mate will empathize with your desire to be surrounded by the beautiful. Sagittarius will be attracted to your illusive, consequently mysterious, qualities. What you will have trouble avoiding are the slough of despondency and the pit of despair. Most of your time will be spent ameliorating your mate's insecurity at best, and self-loathing at worst. Make use of your ability to take the reins without injuring a person's pride. Throw a surprise party in order to bring your self-pitying Sagittarius to life. Or fly away to a Caribbean weekend on the spur of the moment. If all fails, join your mate in his or her favorite pit. You are both capable of surviving the occasional wallow and being the better for it.

LIBRA—CAPRICORN

You are a serious combination of loyalty and stability. You provide the homey security and driving career ambition that you both require. Each of you may be rebuffed and feel emotionally cheated at times, for the warmth that you feel you deserve is not always what you really need. But you're quite a pair. When you are together you are loyal, sturdy and perfectly matched. Conservative and somewhat old-fashioned, you are status-conscious and often slightly insecure about your position. You can symbolize the union of beauty and practicality and your home reflects it. When one of you is unresponsive, the other can't stand it. When one of you is dreamy and unrealistic, there's trouble at home. Don't get caught in someone else's arms either. You are a curious blend of the desire to please other people and the belief that you shouldn't make it too easy for the other person.

If your relationship survived the wild upheavals of the last five years, then you are both greatly changed. Business or personal lives have undergone this radical upheaval, and though life has calmed down, the changes started back then are still developing. You are both more sharply aware of your ambitions and needs, as individuals and as a pair. Your personal selves are undergoing a similar long-term transformation. What keeps your relationship alive is the union of tact and determination. Of all the combinations in the Zodiac, you can see each other through crises as nobody else can.

Hints for Your Capricorn Mate:

Born to please could describe your Capricorn lover. In this partnership you won't have to be ashamed of your social ambitions. Your mate will be charmed by the elegant side of your nature. Looking up is one of Capricorn's favorite occupations, so you are liable to find yourself on a pedestal more often than you like. What may irritate your flowing nature is your mate's fetish for structure and organization. Capricorn's ability to concentrate regardless of the circumstances may drive you up the walls, into the streets, and onto a barstool. Overcome your irritation by becoming part of your mate's concentration. Let him or her put that shrewd commercial mind to work for you. Ask your lover to edit or write your resume. Invite her or him to join you in business meetings. Once you see your Capricorn at work, you'll want to go all the way with your lover.

LIBRA—AQUARIUS

If you want a partnership with strong healthy roots, this can be it. But don't forget that with Aquarius comes the one element you didn't bargain for. Libra will not be able to tolerate wild, flagrant disruption for long. Emotional insecurity or perverse rebelliousness will damage the union. Aquarius cannot allow perpetual domination forever. If freedom is too stringently curtailed, separation is usually the ultimate choice. As a team you come equipped with the unique blend of patience, the capacity to bend, and a certain elasticity when it comes to solving problems that pop up unexpectedly. There is a good humor, a cool, level-headed, detached approach that can allay fears, bring enjoyment, and weather the sudden storms that come up out of nowhere

You can be friends and companions, lovers or husband and wife, but your relationship will have a strange twist, an unusual set of conditions under which it will grow. You can have a turbulent on-again off-again romance, where you never seem to get together at the last minute. You may war between romance and detachment, emotional drama and cool reason, marriage and freedom, but at best you are a friendly pair of lovers. You need maturity, honesty and the sense of duty and responsibility to succeed in this union.

Hints for Your Aquarius Mate:

You've chosen a wild mate this time, at least from an intellectual standpoint. There will be no need to force Aquarius out of pits or down from pedestals. She or he walks a straight line and talks straight from the shoulder. Try not to feel threatened by the Aquarius commitment to truth and beauty. Remember that you too have that commitment, although your style is a more conventional one. Your lover refuses to be tied down to rules or schedules, so it will be to you to introduce order into the relationship. Promise to give up fighting in public if your mate promises to call when she or he is unspeakably late. Schedule organized and intermittent parties for your mate's friends, provided Aquarius stops draging them in at odd hours of the day and night. Present your needs as civil liberties; your Aquarius will respect them. Don't dig too deeply, and your love will last.

LIBRA—PISCES

You are a romantic pair of idealists. Linked through the areas of marriage, sacrifice, work, health and sex, yours is a complex involvement. You can both get lost in a sea of indecision and worry, uncertainty and lack of confidence. You can both drift into situations that smack of escapism and self-indulgence, a kind of passive self-destructiveness that can get you both in trouble. With your love of relationships and intrigue you could get yourselves into quite a messy scene, either personally or professionally. You could fool each other and yourselves, mix up your emotions, blind your eyes to facts until you are really hooked, but romance must always be in the air.

You are both shy, gentle people with a desire to make someone else happy. You share a longing to find a true love, and to live peacefully and easily, enjoying all the pleasures of life. You do not want to hurt anyone else consciously. However, you have the unfortunate ability to convince yourselves your fantasy is valid—as long as it answers your desires. Left alone together you lack sufficient zest and aggressiveness to maintain your relationship on a real plane of the tangible, everyday world.

You could be a mixture of reason and imagination, a true union of head and heart. With enough drive, ambition, and discipline, you could produce a work of art that would reflect the grace and true beauty of your spiritual union.

Hints for Your Pisces Mate:

This one could be the great romance. You each are willing to give a certain part of your soul to the other. When Pisces gives it, be sure to show the appropriate emotional response—something on the order of Greek Tragedy will do. Otherwise you will hurt your Pisces mate's feelings. Not hurting his or her feelings will be one of the premises on which your romance is based. With your refinement and sense of fair play, you'll have no trouble in this area. Prepare yourself for Pisces' gloom and doom pronouncements during self-doubts periods. Protect your own fragile position by diving into your work which, most likely, is Pisces' work. Consult your lover about work no matter how depressed, moody, or tearful he or she is. During bad times your mate does not want to be abandoned. If you channel your dependence into work instead of your psyches, you both can swim.

YOUR PROGRESSED SUN

WHAT IS YOUR NEW SIGN?

Your birth Sign, or Sun Sign, is the central core of your whole personality. It symbolizes everything you try to do and be. It is your main streak, your major source of power, vitality and life. But as you live you learn, and as you learn you progress. The element in your horoscope that measures your progress is called the Progressed Sun. It is the symbol of your growth on Earth, and represents new threads that run through your life. The Progressed Sun measures big changes, turning points and major decisions. It will often describe the path you are taking toward the fulfillment of your desires.

Below you will find brief descriptions of the Progressed Sun. According to the table on page 39, find out about your Progressed Sun and see how and where you fit into the cosmic scheme. Each period lasts about 30 years, so watch and see how dramatic these changes turn out to be.

If Your Sun Is Progressing Into—

SCORPIO, your passions and desires are awakened now as you cross the threshold into a world of intense and fertile creativity. Your powers of penetration will never be greater than they are during this segment of your life. Sex and sexuality become your keywords and you come to understand death and life, mortality and immortality.

Now you can slowly transform your entire nature so that you will be like the adult butterfly emerging from its cocoon.

SAGITTARIUS, look up, for your life will be much brighter from now on. You will find great encouragement for living. Your power of learning will increase; religion, travel, and higher learning will enter your life at this time. Though your aims may be unrealistic and overexpansive, you will be buoyed up by good cheer.

CAPRICORN, you will grow more serious during this period. Plans that are unrealistic will come to no good end. You will need to add structure to your life, confront your limitations, and examine the boundaries that govern your particular life circumstances. You'll have to start working harder to get what you want. Success will be yours during this period as long as you climb toward it.

HOW TO USE THE TABLE

Look for your birthday in the following table; then under the appropriate column, find out approximately when your Progressed Sun will lead you to a new sign. From that point on, for 30 years, the thread of your life will run through that sign. Read the definitions on the preceding pages and see exactly how that life thread will develop.

For example, if your birthday is October 8, your Progressed Sun will enter Scorpio around your 16th birthday and will travel through Scorpio until you are 46 years old. Your Progressed Sun will then move into Sagittarius. Reading the definitions of Scorpio and Sagittarius will tell you *much* about your major involvements and interests during those years.

YOUR PROGRESSED SUN

If your birth-day falls:	start looking at SCORPIO at age	start looking at SAGITTARIUS at age	start looking at CAPRICORN at age
Sept. 23-24	30	60	90
25	29	59	89
26	28	58	88
27	27	57	87
28	26	56	86
29	25	55	85
30	24	54	84
Oct. 1	23	53	83
2	22	52	82
3	21	51	81
4	20	50	80
5	19	49	79
6	18	48	78
7	17	47	77
8	16	46	76
9	15	45	75
10	14	44	74
11	13	43	73
12	12	42	72
13	11	41	71
14	10	40	70
15	9	39	69
16	8	38	68
17	7	37	67
18	6	36	66
19	5	35	65
20	4	34	64
21	3	33	63
22	2	32	62
23	1	31	61

LIBRA BIRTHDAYS

Sept. 23	Mickey Rooney, Louise Nevelson
Sept. 24	F. Scott Fitzgerald, Anthony Newley
Sept. 25	Barbara Walters, William Faulkner
Sept. 26	Florence Kelly, George Gershwin
Sept. 27	Jayne Meadows, Sada Thompson
Sept. 28	Marcello Mastroianni, Brigitte Bardot
Sept. 29	Gene Autry, Anita Ekberg
Sept. 30	Truman Capote, Deborah Kerr
Oct. 1	Marc Edmund Jones, Bonnie Parker
Oct. 2	Groucho Marx, Cissy Farenthold
Oct. 3	Thomas Wolfe, Emily Post
Oct. 4	Buster Keaton
Oct. 5	Chester A. Arthur, Glynis Johns
Oct. 6	Carole Lombard, Jenny Lind
Oct. 7	Elizabeth Janeway, Rita Hayworth
Oct. 8	Eddie Rickenbacker, Emily Blackwell
Oct. 9	Cervantes, John Lennon
Oct. 10	Helen Hayes, Thelonius Monk
Oct. 11	Eleanor Roosevelt, Maria Bueno
Oct. 12	Aleister Crowley, Perle Mesta
Oct. 13	Laraine Day, Molly Pitcher
Oct. 14	Dwight Eisenhower, Katherine Mansfield
Oct. 15	Oscar Wilde, Arthur Schlesinger
Oct. 16	Ben Gurion, Eugene O'Neill
Oct. 17	Jean Arthur, Montgomery Clift
Oct. 18	Lotte Lenya, George C. Scott
Oct. 19	Jack Anderson, John Le Carre
Oct. 20	Art Buchwald, Joyce Brothers
Oct. 21	Samuel Taylor Coleridge, Dizzy Gillespie
Oct. 22	Doris Lessing, Timothy Leary
Oct. 23	Sarah Bernhardt, Johnny Carson

CAN ASTROLOGY
PREDICT THE FUTURE?

Can Astrology really peer into the future? By studying the planets and the stars is it possible to look years ahead and make predictions for our lives? How can we draw the line between ignorant superstition and cosmic mystery? We live in a very civilized world, to be sure. We consider ourselves modern, enlightened individuals. Yet few of us can resist the temptation to take a peek at the future when we think it's possible. Why? What is the basis of such universal curiosity?

The answer is simple. Astrology works, and you don't have to be a magician to find that out. We certainly can't prove astrology simply by taking a look at the astonishing number of people who believe in it, but such figures do make us wonder what lies behind such widespread popularity. The United States alone has more than ten million followers, and in Europe there are 25 million or more. Everywhere in the world hundreds of thousands of serious, intelligent people are charting, studying, and interpreting the positions of the planets and stars every day. Newspaper columns and magazine articles appear daily, broadcasting brief astrological bulletins to millions of curious readers. In Eastern countries, the source of many wisdoms handed down to us from antiquity, Astrology still has a vital place. Why? Surrounded as we are by sophisticated scientific method, how does Astrology, with all its bizarre symbolism and mysterious meaning, survive so magnificently? The answer remains the same. It works.

Nobody knows exactly where astrological knowledge came from. We have references to it dating back to the dawn of human history. Wherever there was a stirring of human consciousness, man began to observe the natural cycles and rhythms that sustained his life. The diversity of human behavior must have been evident even to the first students of consciousness. Yet the basic similarity between members of the human family must have always joined them in the search for some common source, some greater point of origin somehow linked to the heavenly bodies ruling man's whole sense of life and time. The ancient world of Mesopotamia, Chaldea, and Egypt was a highly developed center of astronomical observation and astrological interpretation of heavenly phenomena and their resultant effects on human life.

Amid the seeming chaos of a mysterious unknown universe, man has from earliest times sought to classify, define, and organize the world to which he belongs. Order: that's what the human mind has always striven to maintain in an unceasing battle with its natural counterpart, chaos, or entropy. Men build cities, countries, and empires, subjugating nature to a point of near defeat, and then . . . civilization collapses, empires fall and cities crumble. Nature reclaims the wilderness in the midst of man's monuments to himself and society. Shelly's poem *Ozymandias* is a hymn to the battle between order and chaos. The narrator tells us about a statue, broken, shattered and half-sunk somewhere in the middle of a distant desert. The inscription reads: "Look on my works, ye mighty, and despair." And then we are told: "Nothing beside remains. Round the decay of that colossal wreck, boundless and bare, the lone and level sands stretch far away."

Man has always feared the entropy that seemed to lurk in nature. So he found permanence and constancy in the regular movements of the Sun, Moon and planets and in the positions of the stars. Traditions sprang up from observations of the seasons and crops. Relationships were noted between phenomena in nature and the configurations of the heavenly bodies. This "synchronicity," as it was later called by Carl Jung, extended to thought, mood and behavior, and as such developed the astrological archetypes handed down to us today.

Astrology, a regal science of the stars in the old days, was made available to the king, who was informed of impending events in the heavens, translated of course to their earthly meanings by trusted astrologers. True, astrological knowledge in its infant stages was rudimentary and beset with many superstitions and false premises. But those same dangers exist today in any investigation of occult or mystical subjects. In the East, reverence for Astrology is part of religion. Astrologer-astronomers have held respected positions in government and have taken part in advisory councils on many momentous issues. The duties of the court astrologer, whose office was one of the most important in the land, were clearly defined, as early records show.

Here in our sleek Western world, Astrology glimmers on, perhaps more brilliantly than ever. With all of our technological wonders and complex urbanized environments, we look to Astrology even now to cut through artificiality, dehumanization, and all the materialism of contemporary life, while we gather precious information that helps us live in that material world. Astrology helps us restore balance and get in step with our own rhythms and the rhythms of nature.

The contribution of Astrology to twentieth-century life is more vital than ever. Each new advance in scientific knowledge increases the skill and know-how of our great age. Yet each confirms and develops ancient astrological principles at the same time.

It is usually wise to be a little skeptical and not accept other people's ideas too quickly without thought or examination. Intelligent investigation of Astrology (or the practical application of it) need not mean blind acceptance. We only need to see it working, see our own lives confirming its principles every day, in order to accept and understand it more. To understand ourselves is to know ourselves and to know all. This book can help you to do that—to understand yourself and through understanding develop your own resources and potentials as a rich human being.

YOUR PLACE
AMONG THE STARS

Humanity finds itself at the center of a vast personal universe that extends infinitely outward in all directions. In that sense each is a kind of star radiating, as our Sun does, to all bodies everywhere. These vibrations, whether loving, helpful or destructive, extend outward and generate a kind of "atmosphere" in which woman and man move. The way we relate to everything around us— our joy or our sorrow—becomes a living part of us. Our loved ones and our enemies become the objects of our projected radiations, for better or worse. Our bodies and faces reflect thoughts and emotions much the way light from the Sun reflects the massive reactions occurring deep within its interior. This "light" reaches all who enter its sphere of influence.

All the stars in the sky are sending out vast amounts of energy and light. Their powerful emissions affect every other body everywhere in space. The more science uncovers, the more astonished we become at the complex relationships of all things in the observable universe. Everything is in constant motion and change, yet somehow caught in a gripping attraction almost too awesome to comprehend.

Recent investigations have now uncovered new sources of energy, powerful emitters of different kinds of radiation, such as radio galaxies, pulsars and quasars. These may be almost unimaginably distant bodies, smaller perhaps than a single star, yet brighter than a whole galaxy. Black holes, too, are a recent and mysterious discovery—pockets of dark areas in outer space, perhaps holes in the fabric of our universe through which we might someday travel to other universes. Preposterous? Not at all. Such remote forces could be more strongly linked to us here on Earth than most of us would ever care to think.

Our own personal radiations are just as potent in their own way, really. The reactions that go on deep within us profoundly affect our way of thinking and acting. Our feelings of joy or satisfaction, frustration or anger, must eventually find an outlet. Otherwise we experience the psychological or physiological repercussions of repression. If we can't have a good cry, tell someone our troubles or express love, we soon feel very bad indeed.

As far as our physical selves are concerned, many of us fail to see the direct living relationship between our outer lives, inner reactions and actions, and the effects on our physical body. We all know the feeling of being startled by the sudden ring of a telephone, or the simple frustration of missing a bus. In fact, our minds and bodies are constantly reacting to outside forces. At the same time we, too, are generating actions that will cause a reaction in someone else. You may suddenly decide to phone a friend. If you are a bus driver you might speed along on your way and leave behind an angry would-be passenger. Whatever the case, mind and body are in close communication and they both reflect each other's condition. If you don't believe it, next time you're really angry take a good long look in the mirror!

In terms of human evolution, our ability to understand, control and ultimately change ourselves will naturally affect all of our outside relationships. Astrology is invaluable to helping us comprehend our inner selves. It is a useful tool in helping us retain our integrity, while cooperating with and living in a world full of other human beings.

Let's go back to our original question for a moment. Why is it that even the most wary among us still has a grain of impressionability when it comes to hearing about the future? Everyone would like to part the mysterious veil and see what lies beyond. But even if it is possible to do so, what good can it do us to look years ahead? To know that fully, we must come to an understanding of what the future is.

In simplest terms the future is the natural next step to the present, just as the present is a natural progression from the past. Although our minds can move from one to the other, there is a thread of continuity between past, present and future that joins them together in a coherent sequence. If you are reading this book at this moment, it is the result of a real conscious choice you made in the recent past. That is, you chose to find out what was on these pages, picked up the book and opened it. Because of this choice you may know yourself better in the future. It's as simple as that.

If we could keep our minds clear and free from worry, anxiety and unrealistic wishes, it should be quite possible to predict events and make conclusions about the "synchronicity" of heavenly events and their earthly manifestations. By being totally aware of the present with all its subtle ramifications and clues, the future would be revealed to us with astounding clarity. Knowing ourselves is the key to being able to predict and understand our own future. To learn from past experiences, choices and actions is to fully grasp the present. Coming to grips with the present is to be master of the future.

"Know thyself" is a motto that takes us back to the philosophers of ancient Greece. Mystery religions and cults of initiation throughout the ancient world, schools of mystical discipline, yoga and mental expansion have always been guardians of this one sacred phrase. Know thyself. Of course, that's easy to say. But how do you go about it when there are so many conflicts in our lives and different parts of our personalities? How do we know when we are really "being ourselves" and not merely being influenced by the things we read or see on television, or by the people around us? How can we differentiate the various parts of our character and still remain whole?

There are many methods of classifying human beings into types. Body shapes, muscular types, blood types and genetic types are only a few. Glandular, racial and ethnic divisions can also be observed. Psychology has its own ways of classifying human beings according to their behavior. Some of the most brilliant contributions in this field have been made by Carl Jung, whose profound insight owed much to his knowledge and understanding of astrological processes.

Other disciplines, too, approach the study of human beings from different points of view. Anthropology studies human evolution as the body-mind response to environment. Biology watches physical development and adaptations in body structure. These fields provide valuable information about human beings and the ways they survive, grow and change in their search for their place in eternity. Yet these are all still "branches of science." Until now they have been separate and fragmented. Their contribution has been to provide theories and data, yes, but no lasting solutions to the human problems that have existed since the first two creatures realized they had two separate identities.

It's often difficult to classify yourself according to these different schemes. It's not easy to be objective about yourself. Some things are hard to face; others are hard to see. The different perspectives afforded to us by studying the human organism from all these different disciplines may seem contradictory when they are all really trying to integrate humankind into the whole of the cosmic scheme.

Maybe with the help of Astrology these fields will unite to seek a broader and deeper approach to universal human issues. Astrology's point of view is vast. It transcends racial, ethnic, genetic, environmental and even historical criteria, yet somehow includes them all. Astrology embraces the totality of human experience, then sets about to examine the relationships that are created within that experience.

We don't simply say, "The planets cause this or that." Rather than merely isolating cause or effect, Astrology has unified the ideas of cause and effect. Concepts like past, present and future merge and become, as we shall see a little later on, like stepping-stones across the great stream of Mind. Observations of people and the environment have developed the astrological principles of planetary "influence," but it must be remembered that if there is actual influence, it is mutual. As the planets influence us, so we influence them, for we are forever joined to all past and future motion of the heavenly bodies. This is the foundation of Astrology as it has been built up over the centuries.

ORDER VS. CHAOS

But is it all written in the stars? Is it destined that empires should thrive and flourish, kings reign, lovers love, and then . . . decay, ruin and natural disintegration hold sway? Have we anything to do with determining the cycles of order and chaos? The art of the true astrologer depends on his ability to uncover new information, place it upon the grid of data already collected, and then interpret what he sees as accurate probability in human existence. There may be a paradox here. If we can predict that birds will fly south, could we not, with enough time and samples for observation, determine their ultimate fate when they arrive in the south?

The paradox is that there is no paradox at all. Order and chaos exist together simultaneously in one observable universe. At some remote point in time and space the Earth was formed, and for one reason or another, life appeared here. Whether the appearance of life on planets is a usual phenomenon or an unrepeated accident we can only speculate at this moment. But our Earth and all living things upon its surface conform to certain laws of physical materiality that our observations have led us to write down and contemplate. All creatures, from the one-celled amoeba to a man hurrying home at rush hour, have some basic traits in common. Life in its organization goes from the simple to the complex with a perfection and order that is both awesome and inspiring. If there were no order to our physical world, an apple could turn into a worm and cows could be butterflies.

But the world is an integrated whole, unified with every other part of creation. When nature does take an unexpected turn, we call that a mutation. This is the exciting card in the program of living experience that tells us not everything is written at all. Spontaneity is real. Change is real. Freedom from the expected norm is real. We have seen in nature that only those mutations that can adapt to changes in their environment and continue reproducing themselves will survive. But possibilities are open for sudden transformation, and that keeps the whole world growing.

YOUR HOROSCOPE
AND THE ZODIAC

It's possible that in your own body, as you read this passage, there exist atoms as old as time itself. That's right. You could well be the proud possessor of some carbon and hydrogen (two necessary elements in the development of life) that came into being in the heart of a star billions and billions of years ago. That star could have exploded and cast its matter far into space. This matter could have formed another star, and then another, until finally our Sun was born. From the Sun's fiery mass came the material that later formed the planets—and maybe some of that primeval carbon or hydrogen. That material could have become part of the Earth, part of an early ocean, even early life. These same atoms could well have been carried down to the present day, to this very moment as you read this book. It's really quite possible. You can see how everything is linked to everything else in a most literal way. Of course, we don't know exactly when or how or why the Earth was created. But we do know that it *was* created, and now exists in a gigantic universe that showers it constantly with rays and invisible particles. There is no place we could go on Earth to escape this very real, albeit invisible, cosmic bombardment. You are the point into which all these energies and influences have been focused. You are the prism through which all the light of outer space is being refracted. You are literally a reflection of all the planets and stars.

Your horoscope is a picture of the sky at the moment

of your birth. It's like a gigantic snapshot of the positions of the planets and stars, taken from Earth. Of course the planets never stop moving around the Sun even for the briefest moment, and you represent that motion as it was occurring at the exact hour of your birth at the precise location on the Earth where you were born.

When an astrologer is going to read your chart, he or she asks you for the month, day and year of your birth. She also needs the exact time and place. With this information he sets about consulting various charts and tables in his calculation of the specific positions of the Sun, Moon and stars, relative to your birthplace when you came to Earth. Then he or she locates them by means of the Zodiac.

The Zodiac is a division of the Sun's apparent path into twelve equal divisions, or *signs*. What we are actually dividing up is the Earth's path around the Sun. But from our point of view here on Earth, it seems as if the Sun is making a great circle around our planet in the sky, so we say it's the Sun's apparent path. This twelvefold division, the Zodiac, is like a mammoth address system for any body in the sky. At any given moment, the planets can all be located at a specific point along this path.

How does this affect *you?* Well, a great part of your character—in fact, the central thread of your whole being—is described by that section of the Zodiac that the Sun occupied when you were born. Each sign of the Zodiac has certain basic traits associated with it. Since the Sun remains in each sign for about thirty days, that divides the population into twelve major character types. Of course, not everybody born the same month will have the same character, but you'll be amazed at how many fundamental traits you share with your astrological cousins of the same birth sign, no matter how many environmental differences you boast. The dates on which the Sun changes sign will vary from year to year; that is why many people born near the cusp, or edge, of a sign often have difficulty determining which is their sign without the aid of a professional astrologer who can plot precisely the Sun's apparent motion for any given year. These dates are fluid and change according to the motion of the Earth from year to year.

Here are the twelve signs of the Zodiac as western astrology has recorded them. Listed also are the symbols associated with them and the *approximate* dates when the Sun enters and exits each sign for the year 1996.*

ARIES	Ram	March 20–April 19
TAURUS	Bull	April 19–May 20
GEMINI	Twins	May 20–June 20
CANCER	Crab	June 20–July 22
LEO	Lion	July 22–August 22
VIRGO	Virgin	August 22–September 22
LIBRA	Scales	September 22–October 22
SCORPIO	Scorpion	October 22–November 21
SAGITTARIUS	Archer	November 21–December 21
CAPRICORN	Sea-Goat	December 21–January 20
AQUARIUS	Water-Bearer	January 20–February 19
PISCES	Fish	February 19–March 20

*These dates are fluid and change with the motion of the Earth from year to year.

THE SIGNS OF THE ZODIAC

The signs of the Zodiac are an ingenious and complex summary of human behavioral and physical types, handed down from generation to generation through the bodies of all people in their hereditary material and through their minds. On the following pages you will find brief descriptions of all twelve signs in their highest and most ideal expression.

ARIES
The Sign of the Ram

Aries is the first sign of the Zodiac, and marks the beginning of springtime and the birth of the year. In spring the Earth begins its ascent upward and tips its North Pole toward the Sun. During this time the life-giving force of the Sun streams toward Earth, bathing our planet with the kiss of warmth and life. Plants start growing. Life wakes up. No more waiting. No more patience. The message has come from the Sun: Time to live!

Aries is the sign of the Self and is the crusade for the right of an individual to live in unimpeachable freedom. It represents the supremacy of the human will over all obstacles, limitations and threats. In Aries there is unlimited energy, optimism and daring, for it is the pioneer in search of a new world. It is the story of success and renewal, championship and victory. It is the living spirit of resilience and the power to be yourself, free from all restrictions and conditioning. There is no pattern you *have* to repeat, nobody's rule you just *have* to follow.

Confidence and positive action are born in Aries, and with little thought or fear of the past. Life is as magic as sunrise, with all the creative potential ahead of you for a new day. Activity, energy and adventure characterize this sign. In this sector of the Zodiac there is amazing strength, forthrightness, honesty and a stubborn refusal to accept defeat. The Aries nature is warm-blooded and forgiving, persuasive, masterful and decisive.

In short, Aries is the magic spark of life and being, the source of all initiative, courage, independence and self-esteem.

TAURUS
The Sign of the Bull

Taurus is wealth. It is not just money, property and the richness of material possessions, but also a wealth of the spirit. Taurus rules everything in the visible world we see, touch, hear, smell and taste—the Earth, sea and sky —everything we normally consider "real." It is the sign of economy and reserve, for it is a mixture of thrift and luxury, generosity and practicality. It is a blend of the spiritual and material, for the fertility of the sign is unlimited, and in this sense it is the mystical bank of life. Yet it must hold the fruit of its efforts in its hands and seeks to realize its fantasy-rich imagination with tangible rewards.

Loyalty and *endurance* make this sign perhaps the most stable of all. We can lean on Taurus, count on it, and it makes our earthly lives comfortable, safe and pleasurable. It is warm, sensitive, loving and capable of magnificent, joyful sensations. It is conservative and pragmatic, with a need to be sure of each step forward.

It is the capacity to plan around eventualities without living in the future. Steadfast and constant, this is a sturdy combination of ruggedness and beauty, gentleness and unshakeability of purpose. It is the point at which we join body and soul. Unselfish friend and loyal companion, Taurus is profoundly noble and openly humanitarian. Tenacity and concentration slow the energy down to bring certain long-lasting rewards.

Taurus is a fertile resource and rich ground to grow in, and we all need it for our ideas and plans to flourish. It is the uncut diamond, symbolizing rich, raw tastes and a deep need for satisfaction, refinement and completion.

GEMINI
The Sign of the Twins

Gemini is the sign of mental brilliance. Communication is developed to a high degree of fluidity, rapidity, fluency. It is the chance for expressing ideas and relaying information from one place to another. Charming, debonair and lighthearted, it is a symbol of universal interest and eternal curiosity. The mind is quick and advanced, has a lightning-like ability to assimilate data.

It is the successful manipulation of verbal or visual language and the capacity to meet all events with objectivity and intelligence. It is light, quick wit, with a comic satiric twist. Gemini is the sign of writing or speaking.

It is the willingness to try anything once, with a need to wander and explore, the quick shifting of moods and attitudes being a basic characteristic that indicates a need for change. Versatility is the remarkable Gemini attribute. It is the capacity to investigate, perform and relate over great areas for short periods of time and thus to connect all areas. It is mastery of design and perception, the power to conceptualize and create by putting elements together—people, colors, patterns. It is the reporter's mind, plus a brilliant ability to see things in objective, colorful arrangement. Strength lies in constant refreshment of outlook and joyful participation in all aspects of life.

Gemini is involvement with neighbors, family and relatives, telephones, arteries of news and communication —anything that enhances the human capacity for communication and self-expression. It is active, positive and energetic, with an insatiable hunger for human interchange. Through Gemini bright and dark sides of personality merge and the mind has wings. As it flies it reflects the light of a boundless shining intellect. It is the development of varied talents from recognition of the duality of self.

Gemini is geared toward enjoying life to the fullest by finding, above all else, a means of expressing the inner self to the outside world.

CANCER
The Sign of the Crab

Cancer is the special relationship to *home* and involvement with the family unit. Maintaining harmony in the domestic sphere or improving conditions there is a major characteristic in this sector of the Zodiac. Cancer is attachment between two beings vibrating in sympathy with one another.

It is the comfort of a loving embrace, a tender generosity. Cancer is the place of shelter whenever there are lost or hungry souls in the night. Through Cancer we are fed, protected, comforted and soothed. When the coldness of the world threatens, Cancer is there with gentle understanding. It is protection and understated loyalty, a medium of rich, living feeling that is both psychic and mystical. Highly intuitive, Cancer has knowledge that other signs do not possess. It is the wisdom of the soul.

It prefers the quiet contentment of the home and hearth to the busy search for earthly success and civilized pleasures. Still, there is a respect for worldly knowledge. Celebration of life comes through food. The sign is the muted light of warmth, security and gladness, and its presence means *nourishment*. It rules fertility and the instinct to populate and raise young. It is growth of the soul. It is the ebb and flow of all our tides of feeling, involvements, habits and customs.

Through Cancer is reflected the inner condition of all human beings, and therein lies the seed of knowledge out of which the soul will grow.

LEO

The Sign of the Lion

Leo is love. It represents the warmth, strength and regeneration we feel through love. It is the radiance of lifegiving light and the center of all attention and activity. It is passion, romance, adventure and games. Pleasure, amusement, fun and entertainment are all part of Leo. Based on the capacity for creative feeling and the desire to express love, Leo is the number 1 sign. It represents the unlimited outpouring of all that is warm and positive.

It is loyalty, dignity, responsibility and command. Pride and nobility belong to Leo, and the dashing image of the knight in shining armor, pioneer or hero all are part of Leo. It is a sense of high honor and kingly generosity born out of deep, noble love. It is the excitement of the sportsman, with all the unbeatable flair and style of success. It is a strong, unyielding will and true sense of personal justice, a respect for human freedom and an enlightened awareness of people's needs.

Leo is involvement in the Self 's awareness of personal talents and the desire and need to express them. At best it is forthrightness, courage and efficiency, authority and dignity, showmanship and a talent for organization. Dependable and ardent, the Lion is characterized by individuality, positivism and integrity.

It is the embodiment of human maturity, the effective individual in society, a virile creative force able to take chances and win. It is the love of laughter and the joy of making others happy. Decisive and enthusiastic, the Lion is the creative producer of the Zodiac It is the potential to light the way for others.

VIRGO

The Sign of the Virgin

Virgo is the sign of work and service. It is the symbol of the farmer at harvest time, and represents tireless efforts for the benefit of humanity, the joy of bringing the fruits of the Earth to the table of mankind. Celebration through work is the characteristic of this sign. Sincerity, zeal, discipline and devotion mark the sign of the Virgin.

The key word is *purity*, and in Virgo lies a potential for unlimited self-mastery. Virgo is the embodiment of perfected skill and refined talent. The thread of work is woven into the entire life of Virgo. All creativity is poured into streamlining a job, classifying a system, eradicating unnecessary elements of pure analysis. The true Virgo genius is found in separating the wheat from the chaff.

Spartan simplicity characterizes this sign, and Virgo battles the war between order and disorder. The need to arrange, assimilate and categorize is great; it is the symbol of the diagnostician, the nurse and the healer. Criticism and analysis describe this sign—pure, incisive wisdom and a shy appreciation of life's joys. All is devoted to the attainment of perfection and the ideal of self-mastery.

Virgo is the sign of health and represents the physical body as a functioning symbol of the mental and spiritual planes. It is the state of healing the ills of the human being with natural, temperate living. It is maturation of the ego as it passes from a self-centered phase to its awareness and devotion to humanity.

It is humanitarian, pragmatic and scientific, with boundless curiosity. Focus and clarity of mind are the strong points, while strength of purpose and shy reserve underlie the whole sign. This is separateness, aloofness and solitude for this beacon of the Zodiac. As a lighthouse guides ships, so Virgo shines.

LIBRA
The Sign of the Scales

Libra is the sign of human relationship, marriage, equality and justice. It symbolizes the need of one human being for another, the capacity to find light, warmth and life-giving love in relationship to another human being. It is union on any level—mental, sexual, emotional or business. It is self-extension in a desire to find a partner with whom to share our joys. It is the capacity to recognize the needs of others and to develop to the fullest our powers of diplomacy, good taste and refinement.

Libra is harmony, grace, aesthetic sensibility, and the personification of the spirit of companionship. It represents the skill in maintaining balances and the ability to share mutually of all life's benefits, trials, crises and blessings. Libra is mastery at anticipation of another's needs or reactions. It is the exercise of simple justice with impartial delicacy.

It is the need to relate, to find a major person, place or thing to sustain us and draw out our attention. It is growth through becoming awakened to the outside world and other people. It is the union of two loving souls in honesty, equality, mutual cooperation and mutual accord.

SCORPIO
The Sign of the Scorpion

Scorpio is the sign of dark intensity, swirling passion and sexual magnetism. It is the thirst for survival and primitive animal drives which are the bases of sexual orientation and the creative impulses for self-expression. No other sign has such a profound instinct for survival and reproduction. Out of the abyss of emotions come a thousand creations, each one possessing a life of its own.

Scorpio is completion, determination and endurance, fortified with enough stamina to outlive any enemy. It is the pursuit of goals despite any threat, warning or obstacle that might stand in the way. It simply cannot be stopped. It knows when to wait and when to proceed. It is the constant state of readiness, a vibrant living force that constantly pumps out its rhythm from the depths of being.

Secretive and intimate, Scorpio symbolizes the self-directed creature with a will of steel. It is the flaming desire to create, manipulate and control with a magician's touch. But the most mysterious quality is the capacity for metamorphosis, or total transformation.

This represents supremacy in the battle with dark unseen forces. It is the state of being totally fearless—the embodiment of truth and courage. The healer. It symbolizes the human capacity to face all danger and emerge supreme. As a caterpillar spins its way into the darkness of a cocoon, Scorpio faces the end of existence, says goodbye to an old way of life and goes through a kind of death—or total change.

Then, amid the dread of uncertainty, something remarkable happens. From hopelessness or personal crisis a new individual emerges, like a magnificent butterfly leaving behind its cocoon. It is a human being completely transformed and victorious. This is Scorpio.

SAGITTARIUS
The Sign of the Archer

Sagittarius is the sign of adventure and a thousand and one new experiences. It is the cause and purpose of every new attempt at adventure or self-understanding. It is the embodiment of enthusiasm, search for truth and love of wisdom. Hope and optimism characterize this section of the Zodiac, and it is the ability to leave the past behind and set out again with positive resilience and a happy, cheerful outlook.

It is intelligence and exuberance, youthful idealism and the desire to expand all horizons. It is the constant hatching of dreams, the hunger for knowledge, travel and experience. The goal is exploration itself.

Sagittarius is generosity, humor and goodness of nature, backed up by the momentum of great expectations. It symbolizes the ability of people to be back in the race after having the most serious spills over the biggest hurdles. It is a healthy, positive outlook and the capacity to meet each new moment with unaffected buoyancy.

At this point in the Zodiac, greater conscious understanding begins to develop self-awareness and self-acceptance. It is an Olympian capacity to look upon the bright side and to evolve that aspect of mind we call conscience.

CAPRICORN
The Sign of the Sea-Goat

Capricorn is the sign of structure and physical law. It rules depth, focus and concentration. It is the symbol of success through perseverance, happiness through profundity. It is victory over disruption, and finds reality in codes set up by society and culture. It is the perpetuation of useful, tested patterns and a desire to protect what has already been established.

It is cautious, conservative, conscious of the passage of time, yet ageless. The Goat symbolizes the incorporation of reason into living and depth into loving. Stability, responsibility and fruitfulness through loyalty color this sector of the Zodiac with an undeniable and irrepressible awareness of success, reputation and honor. Capricorn is the culmination of our earthly dreams, the pinnacle of our worldly life.

It is introspection and enlightenment through serious contemplation of the Self and its position in the world. It is mastery of understanding and the realization of dreams.

Capricorn is a winter blossom, a born professional with an aim of harmony and justice, beauty, grace and success. It is the well-constructed pyramid: perfect and beautiful, architecturally correct, mysteriously implacable and hard to know. Highly organized and built on precise foundations to last and last and last. Practical, useful yet magnificent and dignified, signifying permanence and careful planning. Like a pyramid, Capricorn has thick impenetrable walls, complex passageways and false corridors. Yet somewhere at the heart of this ordered structure is the spirit of a mighty ruler.

AQUARIUS

The Sign of the Water-Bearer

Aquarius is the symbol of idealized free society. It is the herding instinct in man as a social animal. It is the collection of heterogeneous elements of human consciousness in coherent peaceful coexistence. Friendship, goodwill and harmonious contact are Aquarius attributes. It is founded on the principle of individual freedom and the brotherly love and respect for the rights of all men and women on Earth.

It is strength of will and purpose, altruism and love of human fellowship. It is the belief in spontaneity and free choice, in the openness to live in a spirit of harmony and cooperation—liberated from restriction, repression and conventional codes of conduct. It is the brilliant capacity to assimilate information instantaneously at the last minute and translate that information into immediate creative action, and thus to live in unpredictability.

This is the progressive mind, the collective mind—groups of people getting together to celebrate life. Aquarius is the child of the future, the utopian working for the betterment of the human race. Funds, charities, seeking better cities and better living conditions for others, involvement in great forms of media or communication, science or research in the hope of joining mankind to his higher self—this is all Aquarius.

It is invention, genius, revolution, discovery—instantaneous breakthrough from limitations. It's a departure from convention, eccentricity, the unexpected development that changes the course of history. It is the discovery of people and all the arteries that join them together. Aquarius is adventure, curiosity, exotic and alien appeal. It pours the water of life and intelligence for all humanity to drink. It is humanism, fraternity and the element of surprise.

PISCES
The Sign of the Fishes

Pisces is faith—undistracted, patient, all-forgiving faith —and therein lies the Pisces capacity for discipline, endurance and stamina.

It is imagination and other-worldliness, the condition of living a foggy, uncertain realm of poetry, music and fantasy. Passive and compassionate, this sector of the Zodiac symbolizes the belief in the inevitability of life. It represents the view of life that everything exists in waves, like the sea. All reality as we know it is a dream, a magic illusion that must ultimately be washed away. Tides pull this way and that, whirlpools and undercurrents sweep across the bottom of life's existence, but in Pisces there is total acceptance of all tides, all rhythms, all possibilities. It is the final resolution of all personal contradictions and all confusing paradoxes.

It is the search for truth and honesty, and the devotion to love, utterly and unquestionably. It is the desire to act with wisdom, kindness and responsibility and to welcome humanity completely free from scorn, malice, discrimination or prejudice. It is total, all-embracing, idealistic love. It is the acceptance of two sides of a question at once and love through sacrifice.

Pisces is beyond reality. We are here today, but may be gone tomorrow. Let the tide of circumstances carry you where it will, for nothing is forever. As all things come, so must they go. In the final reel, all things must pass away. It is deliverance from sorrow through surrender to the infinite. The emotions are as vast as the ocean, yet in the pain of confusion there is hope in the secret cell of one's own heart. Pisces symbolizes liberation from pain through love, faith and forgiveness.

THE SIGNS AND
THEIR KEY WORDS

		Positive	Negative
ARIES	self	courage, initiative, pioneer instinct	brash rudeness, selfish impetuosity
TAURUS	money	endurance, loyalty, wealth	obstinacy, gluttony
GEMINI	mind	versatility, communication	capriciousness, unreliability
CANCER	family	sympathy, homing instinct	clannishness, childishness
LEO	children	love, authority, integrity	egotism, force
VIRGO	work	purity, industry, analysis	fault-finding, cynicism
LIBRA	marriage	harmony, justice	vacillation, superficiality
SCORPIO	sex	survival, regeneration	vengeance, discord
SAGITTARIUS	travel	optimism, higher learning	lawlessness
CAPRICORN	career	depth, responsibility	narrowness, gloom
AQUARIUS	friends	humanity, genius	perverse unpredictability
PISCES	confinement	spiritual love, universality	diffusion, escapism

THE ELEMENTS AND
THE QUALITIES OF THE SIGNS

ELEMENT	SIGN	QUALITY	SIGN
FIRE	ARIES LEO SAGITTARIUS	CARDINAL	ARIES LIBRA CANCER CAPRICORN
EARTH	TAURUS VIRGO CAPRICORN	FIXED	TAURUS LEO SCORPIO AQUARIUS
AIR	GEMINI LIBRA AQUARIUS	MUTABLE	GEMINI VIRGO SAGITTARIUS PISCES
WATER	CANCER SCORPIO PISCES		

Every sign has both an element and a quality associated with it. The element indicates the basic makeup of the sign, and the quality describes the kind of activity associated with each.

Signs can be grouped together according to their *element* and *quality*. Signs of the same element share many basic traits in common. They tend to form stable configurations and ultimately harmonious relationships. Signs of the same quality are often less harmonious, but share many dynamic potentials for growth and profound fulfillment.

THE FIRE SIGNS

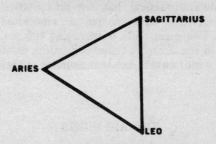

This is the fire group. On the whole these are emotional, volatile types, quick to anger, quick to forgive. They are adventurous, powerful people and act as a source of inspiration for everyone. They spark into action with immediate exuberant impulses. They are intelligent, self-involved, creative and idealistic. They all share a certain vibrancy and glow that outwardly reflects an inner flame and passion for living.

THE EARTH SIGNS

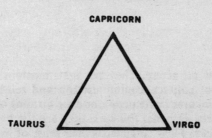

This is the earth group. They are in constant touch with the material world and tend to be conservative. Although they are all capable of spartan self-discipline, they are earthy, sensual people who are stimulated by the tangible, elegant and luxurious. The thread of their lives is always practical, but they do fantasize and are often attracted to dark, mysterious, emotional people. They are like great cliffs overhanging the sea, forever married to the ocean but always resisting erosion from the dark, emotional forces that thunder at their feet.

THE AIR SIGNS

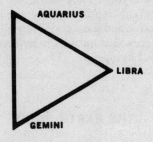

This is the air group. They are light, mental creatures desirous of contact, communication and relationship. They are involved with people and the forming of ties on many levels. Original thinkers, they are the bearers of human news. Their language is their sense of word, color, style and beauty. They provide an atmosphere suitable and pleasant for living. They add change and versatility to the scene, and it is through them that we can explore human intelligence and experience.

THE WATER SIGNS

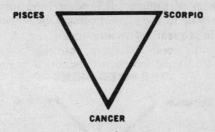

This is the water group. Through the water people, we are all joined together on emotional, non-verbal levels. They are silent, mysterious types whose magic hypnotizes even the most determined realist. They have uncanny perceptions about people and are as rich as the oceans when it comes to feeling, emotion or imagination. They are sensitive, mystical creatures with memories that go back beyond time. Through water, life is sustained. These people have the potential for the depths of darkness or the heights of mysticism and art.

THE CARDINAL SIGNS

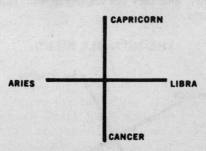

Put together, this is a clear-cut picture of dynamism, activity, tremendous stress and remarkable achievement. These people know the meaning of great change since their lives are often characterized by significant crises and major successes. This combination is like a simultaneous storm of summer, fall, winter and spring. The danger is chaotic diffusion of energy; the potential is irrepressible growth and victory.

THE FIXED SIGNS

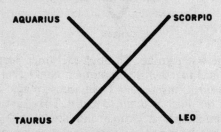

Fixed signs are always establishing themselves in a given place or area of experience. Like explorers who arrive and plant a flag, these people claim a position from which they do not enjoy being deposed. They are staunch, stalwart, upright, trusty, honorable people, although their obstinacy is well-known. Their contribution is fixity, and they are the angels who support our visible world.

THE MUTABLE SIGNS

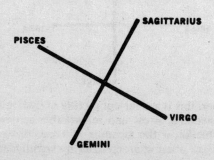

Mutable people are versatile, sensitive, intelligent, nervous and deeply curious about life. They are the translators of all energy. They often carry out or complete tasks initiated by others. Combinations of these signs have highly developed minds; they are imaginative and jumpy and think and talk a lot. At worst their lives are a Tower of Babel. At best they are adaptable and ready creatures who can assimilate one kind of experience and enjoy it while anticipating coming changes.

THE PLANETS AND THE SIGNS THEY RULE

The signs of the Zodiac are linked to the planets in the following way. Each sign is governed or ruled by one or more planets. No matter where the planets are located in the sky at any given moment, they still rule their respective signs. When they travel through the signs they rule, they have special dignity and their effects are stronger.

Following is a list of the planets and the signs they rule. After you read the definitions of the planets from pages 83 to 91, see if you can determine how the planet ruling *your* Sun sign has affected your life.

SIGNS	RULING PLANETS
Aries	Mars, Pluto
Taurus	Venus
Gemini	Mercury
Cancer	Moon
Leo	Sun
Virgo	Mercury
Libra	Venus
Scorpio	Mars, Pluto
Sagittarius	Jupiter
Capricorn	Saturn
Aquarius	Saturn, Uranus
Pisces	Jupiter, Neptune

THE ZODIAC AND
THE HUMAN BODY

The signs of the Zodiac are linked to the human body in a direct relationship. Each sign has a part of the body with which it is associated.

It is traditionally believed that surgery is best performed when the Moon is passing through a sign *other* than the sign associated with the part of the body upon which an operation is to be performed. But often the presence of the Moon in a particular sign will bring the focus of attention to that very part of the body under medical scrutiny.

The principles of medical astrology are complex and beyond the scope of this introduction. We can, however, list the signs of the Zodiac and the parts of the human body connected with them. Once you learn these correspondences, you'll be amazed at how accurate they are.

ARIES	Head, brain, face, upper jaw
TAURUS	Throat, neck, lower jaw
GEMINI	Hands, arms, lungs, nerves
CANCER	Stomach, breasts, womb, liver
LEO	Heart, spine
VIRGO	Intestines, liver
LIBRA	Kidneys, lower back
SCORPIO	Sex and eliminative organs
SAGITTARIUS	Hips, thighs, liver
CAPRICORN	Skin, bones, teeth, knees
AQUARIUS	Circulatory system, lower legs
PISCES	Feet, tone of being

HOW TO APPROXIMATE
YOUR RISING SIGN

Apart from the month and day of birth, the exact time of birth is another vital factor in the determination of an accurate horoscope. Not only do planets move with great speed, but one must know how far the Earth has turned during the day. That way you can determine exactly where the planets are located with respect to the precise birthplace of an individual. This makes your horoscope *your* horoscope. In addition to these factors, another grid is laid upon that of the Zodiac and the planets: the houses. After all three have been considered, specific planetary relationships can be measured and analyzed in accordance with certain ordered procedures. It is the skillful translation of all this complex astrological language that serious astrologers strive for in their attempt at coherent astrological synthesis. Keep this in mind.

The horoscope sets up a kind of framework around which the life of an individual grows like wild ivy, this way and that, weaving its way around the trellis of the natal positions of the planets. The year of birth tells us the positions of the distant, slow-moving planets like Jupiter, Saturn, Uranus and Pluto. The month of birth indicates the Sun sign, or birth sign as it is commonly called, as well as indicating the positions of the rapidly moving planets like Venus, Mercury and Mars. The day of birth locates the position of our Moon, and the moment of birth determines the houses through what is called the Ascendant, or Rising sign.

As the Earth rotates on its axis once every 24 hours,

each one of the twelve signs of the Zodiac appears to be "rising" on the horizon, with a new one appearing about every two hours. Actually it is the turning of the Earth that exposes each sign to view, but you will remember that in much of our astrological work we are discussing "apparent" motion. This Rising sign marks the Ascendant and it colors the whole orientation of a horoscope. It indicates the sign governing the first house of the chart, and will thus determine which signs will govern all the other houses. The idea is a bit complicated at first, and we needn't dwell on complications in this introduction. But if you can imagine two color wheels with twelve divisions superimposed upon each other, one moving slowly and the other remaining still, you will have some idea of how the signs keep shifting the "color" of the houses as the Rising sign continues to change every two hours.

The important point is that the birth chart, or horoscope, actually does define specific factors of a person's makeup. It contains a picture of being, much the way the nucleus of a tiny cell contains the potential for an entire elephant, or a packet of seeds contains a rosebush. If there were no order or continuity to the world, we could plant roses and get elephants. This same order that gives continuous flow to our lives often annoys people if it threatens to determine too much of their lives. We must grow from what we were planted, and there's no reason why we can't do that magnificently. It's all there in the horoscope. Where there is limitation, there is breakthrough; where there is crisis, there is transformation. Accurate analysis of a horoscope can help you find these points of breakthrough and transformation, and it requires knowledge of subtleties and distinctions that demand skillful judgment in order to solve even the simplest kind of personal question.

It is still quite possible, however, to draw some conclusions based upon the sign occupied by the Sun alone.

In fact, if you're just being introduced to this vast subject, you're better off keeping it simple. Otherwise it seems like an impossible jumble, much like trying to read a novel in a foreign language without knowing the basic vocabulary. As with anything else, you can progress in your appreciation and understanding of astrology in direct proportion to your interest. To become really good at it requires study, experience, patience and above all—and maybe simplest of all—a fundamental understanding of what is actually going on right up there in the sky over your head. It is a vital living process you can observe, contemplate and ultimately understand. You can start by observing sunrise, or sunset, or even the Full Moon.

In fact you can do a simple experiment after reading this introduction. You can erect a rough chart by following the simple procedure below. Refer to the diagram on the next page to see what a completed chart for an individual—someone who was born at 5:15 pm on October 31 in New York City—actually looks like. Then follow the steps below to make your own chart.

1. Draw a circle with twelve equal segments.

2. Starting at what would be the nine o'clock position on a clock, number the segments, or houses, from 1 to 12 in a *counterclockwise direction*.

3. Label house number 1 in the following way: 4 A.M. —6 A.M.

4. In a counterclockwise direction, label the rest of the houses: 2 A.M.—4 A.M., Midnight—2 A.M., 10 P.M.— Midnight, 8 P.M.—10 P.M., 6 P.M.—8 P.M., 4 P.M.— 6 P.M.. 2 P.M.—4 P.M., Noon—2 P.M., 10 A.M.—Noon, 8 A.M.— 10 A.M., and 6 A.M.—8 A.M.

5. Now find out what time you were born and place the sun in the appropriate house.

6. Label the edge of that house with your Sun sign.

7. Now label the rest of the houses with the signs,

starting with your Sun sign, in order, still in a *counterclockwise direction*. When you get to Pisces, start over with Aries and keep going until you reach the house behind the Sun.

8. Look to house number 1. The sign that you have now labeled and attached to house number 1 is your Rising sign. It will color your self-image, outlook, physical constitution, early life and whole orientation to life.

When you get through labeling all the houses, your drawing should look something like the diagram below. This diagram was constructed for an individual born at 5:15 P.M. on October 31 in New York City. The Sun is in Scorpio and is found in the 7th house. The Rising sign, or the sign governing house number 1, is Taurus, so this person is a blend of Scorpio and Taurus.

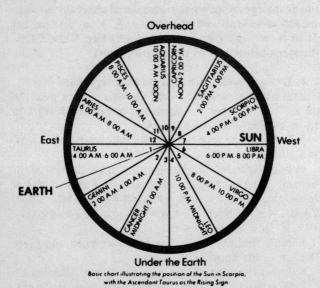

*Basic chart illustrating the position of the Sun in Scorpio,
with the Ascendant Taurus as the Rising Sign.*

Your completed diagram of your own birth chart is, of course, just a mere approximation, since there are many complicated calculations that must be made with respect to adjustments for birth time. If you read descriptions of the sign preceding and the sign following the one you have calculated in the above manner, you may be able to identify yourself better.

Any further calculation would necessitate that you look in an ephemeris, or table of planetary motion, for the positions of the rest of the planets for your particular birth year.

We will leave such mathematics and go on to the next section. There we will list the meanings of the various houses, so you can better understand the position of your Sun. The house where your Sun sign is gives you a description of your basic character and your fundamental drives. You can also see in what areas of life on Earth you will be most likely to focus your constant energy and center your activity.

In the section after the houses, we will also take the time to define briefly all the known planets of our Solar System, the Sun, and the Moon, to acquaint you with more of the astrological vocabulary that you will be meeting again and again.

THE HOUSES AND
THEIR MEANINGS

The twelve houses of every horoscope represent areas of life on Earth, or regions of worldly experience. Depending on which sign of the Zodiac was rising on the eastern horizon at the moment of birth, the activity of each house will be "colored" by the zodiacal sign on its cusp, or edge. In other words, the sign falling on the first house will determine what signs will fall on the rest of the houses.

1   The first house determines the basic orientation to all of life on Earth. It indicates the body type, face, head and brain. It rules your self-image, or the way others see you because of the way you see your self. This is the Ascendant of the horoscope and is the focus of energies of your whole chart. It acts like a prism through which all of the planetary light passes and is reflected in your life. It colors your outlook and influences everything you do and see.

2   This is the house of finances. Here is your approach to money and materialism in general. It indicates where the best sources are for you to improve your financial condition and your earning power as a whole. It describes your values, alliances and assets.

3   This is the house of the day-to-day mind. Short trips, communication and transportation are associated with this house. It deals with routines, brothers and sisters, relatives, neighbors and the near environment at hand. Language, letters and the tools for transmitting information are included in third-house matters.

4   This is the house that describes your home and

homelife, parents, and childhood in the sense of indicating the kind of roots you come from. It symbolizes your present home and domestic situation and reflects your need for privacy and retreat from the world, indicating, of course, what kind of scene you require.

5   Pleasure, love affairs, amusements, parties, creativity, children. This is the house of passion and courtship and of expressing your talents, whatever they are. It is related to the development of your personal life and the capacity to express feeling and enjoy romance.

6   This is the house of work. Here there are tasks to be accomplished and maladjustments to be corrected. It is the house of health as well, and describes some of the likely places where physical health difficulties may appear. It rules routines, regimen, necessary jobs as opposed to a chosen career, army, navy, police—people employed, co-workers and those in service to others. It indicates the individual's ability to harvest the fruit of his own efforts.

7   This is the house of marriage, partnership and unions. It represents the alter ego, all people other than yourself, open confrontation with the public. It describes your partner and the condition of partnership as you discern it. In short, it is your "take" on the world. It indicates your capacity to make the transition from courtship to marriage and specifically what you seek out in others.

8   This is the house of deep personal transition, sex as a form of mutual surrender and interchange between human beings. It is the release from tensions and the completion of the creative processes. The eighth house also has to do with taxes, inheritances and the finances of others, as well as death as the ending of cycles and crises.

9 This is the house of the higher mind, philosophy, religion and the expression of personal conscience through moral codes. It indicates religious leanings, ethical views and the capacity of the individual for a broader perspective and deeper understanding of himself. It is through the ninth house that you make great strides in learning and travel to distant places and come to know yourself through study, dreams and wide experience.

10 This is the house of career, honor and prestige. It marks the culmination of worldly experience and indicates the highest point you can reach, what you look up to, and how high you can go in this lifetime. It describes your parents, employers and how you view authority figures in general, the condition and direction of your profession and your position in the community.

11 This is the house of friendships. It describes your social behavior, your views on humanity and your hopes, aspirations and wishes for an ideal life. It will indicate what kinds of groups, clubs, organizations and friendships you tend to form and what you seek out in your chosen alliances other than with your mate or siblings. This house suggests the capacity for the freedom and unconventionality that an individual is seeking, his sense of his connection with mankind and the definition of his goals, personal and social.

12 This is the house of seclusion, secret wisdom and self-incarceration. It indicates our secret enemies as well, in the sense that there may be persons, feelings or memories we are trying to escape. It is self-undoing in that this house acts against the ego in order to find a higher, more universal purpose. It rules prisons, hospitals, charities and selfless service. It is the house of unfinished psychic business.

THE PLANETS OF THE SOLAR SYSTEM

Here are the planets of the Solar System. They all travel around the Sun at different speeds and different distances. Taken with the Sun, they all distribute individual intelligence and ability throughout the entire chart.

The planets modify the influence of the Sun in a chart according to their own particular natures, strengths and positions. Their positions must be calculated for each year and day, and their function and expression in a horoscope will change as they move from one area of the Zodiac to another.

Following, you will find brief statements of their pure meanings.

THE SUN

The Sun is the center of existence. Around this flaming sphere all the planets revolve in endless orbits. Our star is constantly sending out its beams of light and energy without which no life on Earth would be possible. In astrology it symbolizes everything we are trying to become, the center around which all of our activity in life will always revolve. It is the symbol of our basic nature and describes the natural and constant thread that runs through everything that we do from birth to death on this planet.

THE SUN

Everything in the horoscope ultimately revolves

around this singular body. Although other forces may be prominent in the charts of some individuals, still the Sun is the total nucleus of being and symbolizes the complete potential of every human being alive. It is vitality and the life force. Your whole essence comes from the position of the Sun.

You are always trying to express the Sun according to its position by house and sign. Possibility for all development is found in the Sun, and it marks the fundamental character of your personal radiations all around you.

It symbolizes strength, vigor, ardor, generosity and the ability to function effectively as a mature individual and a creative force in society. It is consciousness of the gift of life. The undeveloped solar nature is arrogant, pushy, undependable and proud, and is constantly using force.

MERCURY

Mercury is the planet closest to the Sun. It races around our star, gathering information and translating it to the rest of the system. Mercury represents your capacity to understand the desires of your own will and to translate those desires into action.

MERCURY

In other words it is the planet of Mind and the power of communication. Through Mercury we develop an ability to think, write, speak and observe—to become aware of the world around us. It colors our attitudes and vision of the world, as well as our capacity to communicate our inner responses to the outside world. Some people who have serious disabilities in their power of verbal communication have often wrongly been described as people lacking intelligence.

Although this planet (and its position in the horoscope) indicates your power to communicate your thoughts and perceptions to the world, intelligence is something deeper. Intelligence is distributed throughout all the planets. It is the relationship of the planets to each other that truly describes what we call intelligence. Mercury rules speaking, language, mathematics, draft and design, students, messengers, young people, offices, teachers and any pursuits where the mind of man has wings.

VENUS

Venus is beauty. It symbolizes the harmony and radiance of a rare and elusive quality: beauty itself. It is refinement and delicacy, softness and charm. In astrology it indicates grace, balance and the esthetic sense. Where Venus is we see beauty, a gentle drawing in of energy and the need for satisfaction and completion. It is a special touch that finishes off rough edges.

VENUS

Venus is the planet of sensitivity, and affection, and it is always the place for that other elusive phenomenon: love. Venus describes our sense of what is beautiful and loving. Poorly developed, it is vulgar, tasteless and self-indulgent. But its ideal is the flame of spiritual love—Aphrodite, goddess of love, and the sweetness and power of personal beauty.

MARS

Mars is raw, crude energy. The planet next to Earth but outward from the Sun is a fiery red sphere that charges through the horoscope with force and fury. It represents the way you reach out for new adventure and new experience. It is energy and drive, initiative, courage and daring. The power to start something and see it through. It can be thoughtless, cruel and wild, angry and hostile, causing cuts, burns, scalds and wounds. It can stab its way through a chart, or it can be the symbol of healthy spirited adventure, well-channeled constructive power to begin and keep up the drive.

MARS

If you have trouble starting things, if you lack the get-up-and-go to start the ball rolling, if you lack aggressiveness and self-confidence, chances are there's another planet influencing your Mars. Mars rules soldiers, butchers, surgeons, salespeople—in general any field that requires daring, bold skill, operational technique or self-promotion.

JUPITER

Jupiter is the largest planet of the Solar System. Scientists have recently learned that Jupiter reflects more light than it receives from the Sun. In a sense it is like a star itself. In astrology it rules good luck and good cheer, health, wealth, optimism, happiness, success and joy. It is the symbol of opportunity and always opens the way for new possibilities in your life. It rules exuberance, enthusiasm, wisdom, knowledge, generosity and all forms of expansion in general. It rules actors, statesmen, clerics, professional people, religion, publishing and the distribution of many people over large areas.

JUPITER

Sometimes Jupiter makes you think you deserve everything, and you become sloppy, wasteful, careless and rude, prodigal and lawless, in the illusion that nothing can ever go wrong. Then there is the danger of your showing overconfidence, exaggeration, undependability and overindulgence.

Jupiter is the minimization of limitation and the emphasis on spirituality and potential. It is the thirst for knowledge and higher learing.

SATURN

Saturn circles our system in dark splendor with its mysterious rings, forcing us to be awakened to whatever we have neglected in the past. It will present real puzzles and problems to be solved, causing delays, obstacles and hindrances. By doing so, Saturn stirs our own sensitivity to those areas where we are laziest.

SATURN

Here we must patiently develop *method*, and only through painstaking effort can our ends be achieved. It brings order to a horoscope and imposes reason just where we are feeling least reasonable. By creating limitations and boundary, Saturn shows the consequences of being human and demands that we accept the changing cycles inevitable in human life. Saturn rules time, old age and sobriety. It can bring depression, gloom, jealousy and greed, or serious acceptance of responsibilities out of which success will develop. With Saturn there is nothing to do but face facts. It rules laborers, stones, granite, rocks and crystals of all kinds.

THE OUTER PLANETS:
URANUS, NEPTUNE, PLUTO

Uranus, Neptune, and Pluto are the outer planets. They liberate human beings from cultural conditioning, and in that sense are the law breakers. In early times it was thought that Saturn was the last planet of the system—the outer limit beyond which we could never go. The discovery of the next three planets ushered in new phases of human history, revolution and technology.

URANUS

Uranus rules unexpected change, upheaval, revolution. It is the symbol of total independence and asserts the freedom of an individual from all restriction and restraint. It is a breakthrough planet and indicates talent, originality and genius in a horoscope. It usually causes last-minute reversals and changes of plan, unwanted separations, accidents, catastrophes and eccentric behavior. It can add irrational rebelliousness and perverse bohemianism to a personality or a streak of unaffected brilliance in science and art.

URANUS

Uranus rules technology, aviation and all forms of electrical and electronic advancement. It governs great leaps forward and topsy-turvy situations, and *always* turns things around at the last minute. Its effects are difficult to ever really predict, since it rules sudden last-minute decisions and events that come like lightning out of the blue.

NEPTUNE

Neptune dissolves existing reality the way the sea erodes the cliffs beside it. Its effects are subtle like the ringing of a buoy's bell in the fog. It suggests a reality higher than definition can usually describe. It awakens a sense of higher responsibility often causing guilt, worry, anxieties or delusions. Neptune is associated with all forms of escape and can make things seem a certain way so convincingly that you are absolutely sure of something that eventually turns out to be quite different.

NEPTUNE

It is the planet of illusion and therefore governs the invisible realms that lie beyond our ordinary minds, beyond our simple factual ability to prove what is "real." Treachery, deceit, disillusionment and disappointment are linked to Neptune. It describes a vague reality that promises eternity and the divine, yet in a manner so complex that we cannot really fathom it at all. At its worst Neptune is a cheap intoxicant; at its best it is the poetry, music and inspiration of the higher planes of spiritual love. It has dominion over movies, photographs and much of the arts.

PLUTO

Pluto lies at the outpost of our system and therefore rules finality in a horoscope—the final closing of chapters in your life, the passing of major milestones and points of development from which there is no return. It is a final wipeout, a closeout, an evacuation. It is a distant, subtle but powerful catalyst in all transformations that occur. It creates, destroys, then recreates. Sometimes Pluto starts its influence with a minor event or insignificant incident that might even go unnoticed. Slowly but surely, little by little, everything changes, until at last there has been a total transformation in the area of your life where Pluto has been operating. It rules mass thinking and the trends that society first rejects, then adopts and finally outgrows.

PLUTO

Pluto rules the dead and the underworld—all the powerful forces of creation and destruction that go on all the time beneath, around and above us. It can bring a lust for power with strong obsessions.

It is the planet that rules the metamorphosis of the caterpillar into a butterfly, for it symbolizes the capacity to change totally and forever a person's life style, way of thought and behavior.

THE MOON

Exactly how does the Moon affect us psychologically and psychically? We know it controls the tides; we've already seen that. We understand how it affects blood rhythm and body tides, together with all the chemical fluids that constitute our physical selves. Astronauts have walked upon its surface, and our scientists are now studying and analyzing data that will help determine the age of our satellite, its origin and makeup.

THE MOON

But the true mystery of that small body as it circles our Earth each month remains hidden. Is it really a dead, lifeless body that has no light or heat of its own, reflecting only what the gigantic Sun throws toward it? Is it a sensitive reflecting device, which translates the blinding, billowing energy from our star into a language our bodies can understand?

In Astrology, the Moon is said to rule our feelings, customs, habits and moods. As the Sun is the constant, ever shining source of life in daytime, the Moon is our nighttime *mother,* lighting up the night and swiftly moving, reflecting ever so rapidly the changing phases of behavior and personality. If we feel happy or joyous, or we notice certain habits and repetitive feelings that bubble up from our dark centers then vanish as quickly as they appeared, very often it is the position of the Moon that describes these changes.

THE MOON IN ALL SIGNS

The Moon moves quickly through the Zodiac, that is, through all twelve signs of our Sun's apparent path. It takes approximately one month for the entire trip, staying in each sign for about 2½ days. During its brief stay in a given sign, the moods and responses of people are always colored by the nature of that sign, any planets located there at that time, or any other heavenly bodies placed in such a way that the Moon will pick up their "vibration" as well. It's astonishing to observe how clearly the Moon changes people's interests and involvements as it moves along.

The following section gives brief descriptions of the Moon's influence in each sign.

MOON IN ARIES

There's excitement in the air. Some new little thing appears, and people are quick and full of energy and enterprise, ready for something new and turning on to a new experience. There's not much patience for hesitation, doubt or preoccupation with guilty self-damning recriminations. What's needed is action. People feel like putting their plans into operation. Pleasure and adventure characterize the mood, and it's time for things to change, pick up, improve. Confidence, optimism and positive feeling pervade the air. Sick people take a turn for the better. Life stirs with a feeling of renewal. People react bravely to challenges, with a sense of courage and dynamism. Self-reliance is the key word, and people minimize their problems and maximize the power to exercise freedom of the will. There is an air of abruptness and shortness of consideration, but, at the same time, people are feeling the courage of their convictions to do something for themselves. Feelings are strong and intuitive, and the mood is idealistic and freedom-oriented.

MOON IN TAURUS

Here the mood is just as pleasure loving, but less idealistic. Now the concerns are more materialistic, money-oriented and down-to-earth. The mood is more stable, diligent, thoughtful and deliberate. It is a time when feelings are rich and deep, with a profound appreciation of the good things the world has to offer and the pleasures of the sensations. It is a period when people's minds are more serious, "realistic," and devoted to the increases and improvements of property and possessions and acquisition of wealth. It's a much more conservative tone, and people are more fixed in their views, sedentary and needing to add to their stability in every way. Assessment of assets, criticism and the execution of tasks are strong involvements of the Taurus Moon when financial matters demand attention. It is devotion to security on a financial and emotional level. It is a fertile time, when ideas can begin to take root and grow.

MOON IN GEMINI

There is a rapid increase in movement. People are moving around, exchanging ideas and information. Gossip and news travel fast under this Moon, because people are naturally involved with communication, finding out things from some, passing on information to others. Feelings shift to a more mental level now, and people feel and say things that are sincere at the moment but lack the root and depth to endure much beyond the moment. People are involved with short-term engagements, quick trips from here to there, and there is a definite need for changing the scene. You'll find people flirtatious and talkative, experimental and easygoing, falling into encounters they hadn't planned on. The mind is quick and active, with powers of writing and speaking greatly enhanced. Radio, television, letters, newspapers and magazines are in the spotlight with the Moon in Gemini, and new chances pop up for self-expression, with new people involved. Relatives and neighbors are tuned in to you and you to them. Take advantage of this fluidity of mind. It can rescue you from worldly involvements and get you into new surroundings for a short while.

MOON IN CANCER

Now you'll see people heading home. People are more likely to turn their attention inward to their place of residence under this position of the Moon. The active, changeable moods of yesterday vanish, and people settle in as if they were searching for a nest of security.

Actually people are retiring now, seeking to find peace and quiet within themselves. That's what they're feeling when they prefer to stay home rather than go out with a whole crowd of people to strange places. They need the warmth and comfort of the family and hearth. Maybe they feel anxious and insecure from the hustle and bustle of the workaday world. Maybe they're just "tired." But it's definitely a time of more tender need for emotional sustenance. It's a time for nostalgia and returning to times and places that once nourished you deeply. Thoughts of parents, family and old associations come to people. The heritage of their family ties holds them strongly now. These are personal needs that must be fed. Moods are deep and mysterious and sometimes sad. People are silent, psychic and imaginative during this period. It's a fruitful time when people respond to love, food and all the comforts of the inner world.

MOON IN LEO

The shift is back out in the world, and people are born again, like kids. They feel zestful, passionate, exuberant and need plenty of attention. They're interested in having a good time, enjoying themselves, and the world of entertainment takes over for a while. Places of amusement, theaters, parties, sprees, a whole gala of glamorous events, characterize this stage of the Moon's travel. Gracious, lavish hosting and a general feeling of buoyancy and flamboyance are in the air. It's a time of sunny, youthful fun when people are in the mood to take chances and win. The approach is direct, ardent and strong. Bossy, authoritarian feelings predominate, and people throw themselves forward for all they're worth. Flattery is rampant, but the ego is vibrant and flourishing with the kiss of life, romance and love. Speculation is indicated, and it's usually a time to go out and try your hand at love. Life is full and rich as a summer meadow, and feelings are warm.

MOON IN VIRGO

The party's over. Eyelashes are on the table. This is a time for cleaning up after the merrymakers have gone home. People are now concerned with sobering up and getting personal affairs straight, clearing up any confusions or undefined feelings from the night before, and generally attending to the practical business of doctoring up after the party. People are back at work, concerned with necessary, perhaps tedious tasks—paying bills, fixing and adjusting things and generally purifying their lives, streamlining their affairs and involving themselves with work and service to the community. Purity is the key word in personal habits, diet and emotional needs. Propriety and coolness take the place of yesterday's devil-may-care passion, and the results are a detached, inhibited period for the Moon. Feelings are not omitted; they are merely subjected to the scrutiny of the mind and thus purified. Health comes to the fore, and people are interested in clearing up problems.

MOON IN LIBRA

Here there is a mood of harmony, when people strive to join with other people in a bond of peace and justice. At this time people need relationships and often seek the company of others in a smooth-flowing feeling of love, beauty and togetherness. People make efforts to understand other people, and though it's not the best time to make decisions, many situations keep presenting themselves from the outside to change plans and offer new opportunities. There is a general search for accord between partners, and differences are explored as similarities are shared. The tone is concilatory, and the mood is one of cooperation, patience and tolerance. People do not generally feel independent, and sometimes this need to share or lean on others disturbs them. It shouldn't. This is the moment for uniting and sharing, for feeling a mutual flow of kindness and tenderness between people. The air is ingratiating and sometimes lacks stamina, courage and a consistent, definite point of view. But it is a time favoring the condition of beauty and the development of esthetics.

MOON IN SCORPIO

This is not a mood of sharing. It's driving, intense, brooding and full of passion and desire. Its baser aspects are the impulses of selfishness, cruelty, and the pursuit of animal drives and appetites. There is a craving for excitement and a desire to battle and win in a bloodthirsty war for survival. It is competitive and ruthless, sarcastic and easily bruised, highly sexual and touchy, without being especially tender. Retaliation, jealousy and revenge can be felt too during this time. Financial involvements, debts and property issues arise now. Powerful underworld forces are at work here, and great care is needed to transform ignorance into wisdom, to keep the mind from descending into the lower depths. During the Moon's stay in Scorpio we contact the dark undercurrents swirling around and get in touch with a magical part of our natures. Interest lies in death, inheritance and the powers of rebirth and regeneration.

MOON IN SAGITTARIUS

Here the mind climbs out of the depths, and people are involved with the higher, more enlightened and conscious facets of their personality. There's a renewed interest in learning, education and philosophy, with a new involvement with ethics, morals, national and international issues: a concern with looking for a better way to live. It's a time of general improvement, with people feeling more deeply hopeful and optimistic. They are dreaming of new places, new possibilities, new horizons. They are emerging from the abyss and leaving the past behind, with their eyes out toward the new horizon. They decide to travel, or renew their contacts with those far away. They question their religious beliefs and investigate new areas of metaphysical inquiry. It's a time for adventure, sports, playing the field—people have their eye on new possibilities. They are bored with depression and details. They feel restless and optimistic, joyous and delighted to be alive. Thoughts revolve around adventure, travel, liberation.

MOON IN CAPRICORN

When the Moon moves into Capricorn things slow

down considerably. People require a quieter, more organized and regularized condition. Their minds are sober, more "realistic," and they are methodically going about bringing their dreams and plans into reality. They are more conscious of what is standing between them and success, and during this time they take definite, decisive steps to remove any obstacles from their path. They are cautious, suspicious, sometimes depressed, discouraged and gloomy, but they are more determined than ever to accomplish their tasks. They take care of responsibilities now, wake up to facts, and wrestle with problems and dilemmas of this world. They are politically minded and concerned with social convention now, and it is during this period that conditioning and conformity elicit the greatest responses. People are moderate and serious and surround themselves with what is most familiar. They want predictable situations and need time to think deeply and deliberately about all issues. It's a time for planning.

MOON IN AQUARIUS

Spontaneity replaces the sober predictability of yesterday. Now events, people and situations pop up, and you take advantage of unsought opportunities and can expect the unexpected. Surprises, reversals, and shifts in plans mark this period. There is a resurgence of optimism, and things you wouldn't expect to happen suddenly do. What you were absolutely sure was going to happen, simply doesn't. Here there is a need for adventure born from a healthy curiosity that characterizes people's moods. Unrealistic utopias are dreamed of, maybe, and it is from such idealistic dreams that worlds of the future are built. There is a renewed interest in friendship, comradeship, brotherly love and union on high planes of mental and spiritual companionship. People free each other from grudges or long-standing deadlocks, and there is a hopeful joining of hands in a spirit of love and peace. People don't feel like sticking to previous plans and they need to be able to respond to new situations at the last minute. People need freedom. Groups of people come together and meet, perhaps for a common purpose like having dinner or hearing music, and leave knowing each other better.

MOON IN PISCES

Flashes of brilliant insight and mysterious knowledge characterize this stage of the Moon's passage through the Zodiac. Sometimes valuable "truths" seem to emerge which, later in the light of day, turn out to be false. This is a time of poetry, intuition and music, when worldly realities can be the most illusory and unreliable of all. There are often feelings of remorse, guilt or sorrow connected with this Moon—sorrow from the childhood or family or past. Confusion, anxiety, worry and a host of imagined pains and sorrows may drag you down until you cannot move or think. Often there are connections with hospitals, prisons, alcohol, drugs and lower forms of escape. It is a highly emotional time, when the feelings and compassion for humanity and all people everywhere rise to the surface of your being. Mysteries of society and the soul now rise to demand solutions, but often the riddles posed during this period have many answers that all seem right. It is more a time for inner reflection than positive action. It is a time when poetry and music float to the surface of the being, and for the creative artist it is the richest source of his inspiration.

MOON TABLES

Atlanta, Boston, Detroit, Miami, Washington,
Montreal, Ottawa, Quebec, Bogota, Havana,
Lima, Santiago . . . . Same time

Chicago, New Orleans, Houston, Winnipeg, Churchill,
Mexico City. . . . . Deduct 1 hour

Albuquerque, Denver, Phoenix, El Paso,
Edmonton, Helena. . . . . Deduct 2 hours

Los Angeles, San Francisco, Reno, Portland,
Seattle, Vancouver. . . . . Deduct 3 hours

Honolulu, Anchorage, Fairbanks, Kodiak . . . . Deduct 5 hours

Nome, Samoa, Tonga, Midway . . . . Deduct 6 hours

Halifax, Bermuda, San Juan, Caracas, La Paz,
Barbados . . . . Add 1 hour

St. John's, Brasilia, Rio de Janeiro, Sao Paulo,
Buenos Aires, Montevideo . . . . Add 2 hours

Azores, Cape Verde Islands. . . . . Add 3 hours

Canary Islands, Madeira, Reykjavik . . . . Add 4 hours

London, Paris, Amsterdam, Madrid, Lisbon, Gibraltar,
Belfast, Rabat . . . . Add 5 hours

Frankfurt, Rome, Oslo, Stockholm, Prague,
Belgrade . . . . Add 6 hours

Bucharest, Beirut, Tel Aviv, Athens, Istanbul, Cairo,
Alexandria, Cape Town, Johannesburg. . . . . Add 7 hours

Moscow, Leningrad, Baghdad, Dhahran, Addis Ababa,
Nairobi, Teheran, Zanzibar. . . . . Add 8 hours

Bombay, Calcutta, Sri Lanka. Add 10½ hours

Hong Kong, Shanghai, Manila, Peking, Perth . . . . Add 13 hours

Tokyo, Okinawa, Darwin, Pusan . . . . Add 14 hours

Sydney, Melbourne, Port Moresby, Guam . . . . Add 15 hours

Auckland, Wellington, Suva, Wake . . . . Add 17 hours

1996 MOON TABLES—NEW YORK TIME

JANUARY		FEBRUARY		MARCH	
Day Moon Enters		**Day Moon Enters**		**Day Moon Enters**	
1. Gemini	9:30 pm	1. Cancer		1. Leo	11:48 am
2. Gemini		2. Cancer		2. Leo	
3. Gemini		3. Leo	4:47 am	3. Virgo	11:14 pm
4. Cancer	9:57 am	4. Leo		4. Virgo	
5. Cancer		5. Virgo	4:23 pm	5. Virgo	
6. Leo	10:31 pm	6. Virgo		6. Libra	8:41 am
7. Leo		7. Virgo		7. Libra	
8. Leo		8. Libra	2:31 am	8. Scorp.	4:06 pm
9. Virgo	10:30 am	9. Libra		9. Scorp.	
10. Virgo		10. Scorp.	10:36 am	10. Sagitt.	9:33 pm
11. Libra	8:56 pm	11. Scorp.		11. Sagitt.	
12. Libra		12. Sagitt.	3:59 pm	12. Sagitt.	
13. Libra		13. Sagitt.		13. Capric.	1:09 am
14. Scorp.	4:31 am	14. Capric.	6:30 pm	14. Capric.	
15. Scorp.		15. Capric.		15. Aquar.	3:16 am
16. Sagitt.	8:26 am	16. Aquar.	7:01 pm	16. Aquar.	
17. Sagitt.		17. Aquar.		17. Pisces	4:51 am
18. Capric.	9:08 am	18. Pisces	7:10 pm	18. Pisces	
19. Capric.		19. Pisces		19. Aries	7:16 am
20. Aquar.	8:16 am	20. Aries	8:59 pm	20. Aries	
21. Aquar.		21. Aries		21. Taurus	0:00 pm
22. Pisces	8:03 am	22. Aries		22. Taurus	
23. Pisces		23. Taurus	2:09 am	23. Gemini	8:00 pm
24. Aries	10:38 am	24. Taurus		24. Gemini	
25. Aries		25. Gemini	11:15 am	25. Gemini	
26. Taurus	5:17 pm	26. Gemini		26. Cancer	7:07 am
27. Taurus		27. Cancer	11:11 pm	27. Cancer	
28. Taurus		28. Cancer		28. Leo	7:38 pm
29. Gemini	3:43 am	29. Cancer		29. Leo	
30. Gemini				30. Leo	
31. Cancer	4:12 pm			31. Virgo	7:16 am

Summer time to be considered where applicable.

1996 MOON TABLES—NEW YORK TIME

APRIL Day Moon Enters		MAY Day Moon Enters		JUNE Day Moon Enters	
1. Virgo		1. Libra		1. Sagitt	
2. Libra	4:27 pm	2. Scorp.	7:43 am	2. Capric.	9:30 pm
3. Libra		3. Scorp.		3. Capric.	
4. Scorp.	10:58 pm	4. Sagitt.	11:06 am	4. Aquar.	9:46 pm
5. Scorp.		5. Sagitt.		5. Aquar.	
6. Scorp.		6. Capric.	12:55 pm	6. Pisces	11:20 pm
7. Sagitt.	3:22 am	7. Capric.		7. Pisces	
8. Sagitt.		8. Aquar.	2:40 pm	8. Pisces	
9. Capric.	6:31 am	9. Aquar.		9. Aries	3:24 am
10. Capric.		10. Pisces	5:30 pm	10. Aries	
11. Aquar.	9:10 am	11. Pisces		11. Taurus	10:12 am
12. Aquar		12. Aries	10:01 pm	12. Taurus	
13. Pisces	12:01 pm	13. Aries		13. Gemini	7:17 pm
14. Pisces		14. Aries		14. Gemini	
15. Aries	3:44 pm	15. Taurus	4:26 am	15. Gemini	
16. Aries		16. Taurus		16. Cancer	6:09 am
17. Taurus	9:06 pm	17. Gemini	12:49 pm	17. Cancer	
18. Taurus		18. Gemini		18. Leo	6:23 pm
19. Taurus		19. Cancer	11:17 pm	19. Leo	
20. Gemini	4:55 am	20. Cancer		20. Leo	
21. Gemini		21. Cancer		21. Virgo	7:08 am
22. Cancer	3:26 pm	22. Leo	11:29 am	22. Virgo	
23. Cancer		23. Leo		23. Libra	6:38 pm
24. Cancer		24. Virgo	11:59 pm	24. Libra	
25. Leo	3:45 am	25. Virgo		25. Libra	
26. Leo		26. Virgo		26. Scorp.	2:54 am
27. Virgo	3:50 pm	27. Libra	10:34 am	27. Scorp.	
28. Virgo		28. Libra		28. Sagitt.	7:02 pm
29. Virgo		29. Scorp.	5:31 pm	29. Sagitt.	
30. Libra	1:28 am	30. Scorp.		30. Capric.	7:48 pm
		31. Sagitt.	8:44 pm		

Summer time to be considered where applicable.

1996 MOON TABLES—NEW YORK TIME

JULY		AUGUST		SEPTEMBER	
Day Moon Enters		**Day Moon Enters**		**Day Moon Enters**	
1. Capric.		1. Pisces		1. Taurus	7:21 am
2. Aquar.	7:06 am	2. Aries	6:06 pm	2. Taurus	
3. Aquar.		3. Aries		3. Gemini	2:09 pm
4. Pisces	7:08 am	4. Taurus	10:34 pm	4. Gemini	
5. Pisces		5. Taurus		5. Gemini	
6. Aries	9:43 am	6. Taurus		6. Cancer	0:30 am
7. Aries		7. Gemini	6:50 am	7. Cancer	
8. Taurus	3:44 pm	8. Gemini		8. Leo	
9. Taurus		9. Cancer	5:58 pm	9. Leo	12:55 pm
10. Taurus		10. Cancer		10. Leo	
11. Gemini	0:53 am	11. Cancer		11. Virgo	1:29 am
12. Gemini		12. Leo	6:30 am	12. Virgo	
13. Cancer	12:09 pm	13. Leo		13. Libra	12:52 pm
14. Cancer		14. Virgo	7:08 pm	14. Libra	
15. Cancer		15. Virgo		15. Scorp.	10:21 pm
16. Leo	0:32 am	16. Virgo		16. Scorp.	
17. Leo		17. Libra	6:56 am	17. Scorp.	
18. Virgo	1:17 pm	18. Libra		18. Sagitt.	5:32 am
19. Virgo		19. Scorp.	4:51 pm	19. Sagitt.	
20. Virgo		20. Scorp.		20. Capric.	10:13 am
21. Libra	1:15 am	21. Sagitt.	11:49 pm	21. Capric.	
22. Libra		22. Sagitt.		22. Aquar.	12:40 pm
23. Scorp.	10:44 am	23. Sagitt.		23. Aquar.	
24. Scorp.		24. Capric.	3:23 am	24. Pisces	1:44 pm
25. Sagitt.	4:25 pm	25. Capric.		25. Pisces	
26. Sagitt.		26. Aquar.	4:11 am	26. Aries	2:47 pm
27. Capric.	6:18 pm	27. Aquar.		27. Aries	
28. Capric.		28. Pisces	3:50 am	28. Taurus	5:25 pm
29. Aquar.	5:48 pm	29. Pisces		29. Taurus	
30. Aquar.		30. Aries	4:16 am	30. Gemini	11:02 pm
31. Pisces	5:02 pm	31. Aries			

Summer time to be considered where applicable.

1996 MOON TABLES—NEW YORK TIME

OCTOBER		NOVEMBER		DECEMBER	
Day Moon Enters		**Day Moon Enters**		**Day Moon Enters**	
1. Gemini		1. Cancer		1. Leo	
2. Gemini		2. Leo	4:17 am	2. Virgo	1:12 am
3. Cancer	8:15 am	3. Leo		3. Virgo	
4. Cancer		4. Virgo	4:58 pm	4. Libra	1:24 pm
5. Leo	8:13 pm	5. Virgo		5. Libra	
6. Leo		6. Virgo		6. Scorp.	10:40 pm
7. Leo		7. Libra	4:30 am	7. Scorp.	
8. Virgo	8:50 am	8. Libra		8. Scorp.	
9. Virgo		9. Scorp.	1:03 pm	9. Sagitt.	3:59 am
10. Libra	8:01 pm	10. Scorp.		10. Sagitt.	
11. Libra		11. Sagitt.	6:27 pm	11. Capric.	6:15 am
12. Libra		12. Sagitt.		12. Capric.	
13. Scorp.	4:47am	13. Capric.	9:45 pm	13. Aquar.	7:15 am
14. Scorp.		14. Capric.		14. Aquar.	
15. Sagitt.	11:08 am	15. Capric.		15. Pisces	8:45 am
16. Sagitt.		16. Aquar.	0:15 am	16. Pisces	
17. Capric.	3:38 pm	17. Aquar.		17. Aries	11:56 am
18. Capric.		18. Pisces	3:01 am	18. Aries	
19. Aquar.	6:52 pm	19. Pisces		19. Taurus	5:11 pm
20. Aquar.		20. Aries	6:35 am	20. Taurus	
21. Pisces	9:23 pm	21. Aries		21. Taurus	
22. Pisces		22. Taurus	11:13 am	22. Gemini	0:18 am
23. Aries	11:51 pm	23. Taurus		23. Gemini	
24. Aries		24. Gemini	5:21 pm	24. Cancer	9:15 am
25. Aries		25. Gemini		25. Cancer	
26. Taurus	3:12 am	26. Gemini		26. Cancer	
27. Taurus		27. Cancer	1:38 am	27. Leo	3:03 pm
28. Gemini	8:36 am	28. Cancer		28. Leo	
29. Gemini		29. Leo	12:31 pm	29. Virgo	8:46 am
30. Cancer	4:57 pm	30. Leo		30. Virgo	
31. Cancer				31. Libra	9:33 pm

Summer time to be considered where applicable.

1996 PHASES OF THE MOON—NEW YORK TIME

New Moon	First Quarter	Full Moon	Last Quarter
Dec. 5 ('95)	Dec. 28 ('95)	Jan. 5	Jan. 13
Jan. 20	Jan. 27	Feb. 4	Feb. 12
Feb. 18	Feb. 25	Mar. 4	Mar. 12
Mar. 19	Mar. 26	Apr. 3	Apr. 10
Apr. 17	Apr. 25	May 3	May 10
May 17	May 25	June 1	June 8
June 15	June 24	June 30	July 7
July 15	July 23	July 30	Aug. 6
Aug. 14	Aug. 21	Aug. 28	Sep. 4
Sep. 12	Sept. 20	Sept. 26	Oct. 4
Oct. 12	Oct. 19	Oct. 26	Nov. 3
Nov. 10	Nov. 17	Nov. 24	Dec. 3
Dec. 10	Dec. 17	Dec. 24	Jan. 2 ('97)

Each phase of the Moon lasts approximately seven to eight days, during which the Moon's shape gradually changes as it comes out of one phase and goes into the next.

There will be a partial solar eclipse during the New Moon phase on April 17 and October 12. There will be a lunar eclipse during the Full Moon phase on April 3 and September 26.

Use the Moon phases to connect you with your lucky numbers for this year. See page 107 and your lucky numbers.

1996 FISHING GUIDE

	Good	Best
January	2-3-4-7-8-20	5-6-13-27
February	3-4-5-6-7-12-18-25	1-2
March	2-3-4-5-6-12-19	7-8-27
April	1-2-7-17-25	3-4-5-6-10-30
May	4-5-6-10-17-25	1-2-3-29-30-31
June	1-2-16-28-29-30	3-4-8-24
July	2-3-4-7-27-30-31	1-15-23-28-29
August	14-22-26-27-30-31	1-2-6-25-28-29
September	4-12-20-24-26-27-28	25-29-30
October	24-25-28-29	4-12-19-23-26-27
November	3-22-25-26	11-18-23-24-27-28
December	3-10-17-22-23-24-27	21-25-26

1996 PLANTING GUIDE

	Aboveground Crops	Root Crops	Pruning	Weeds Pests
January	1-23-27-28	6-12-13-14-15-19	6-14-15	7-8-9-10-11-17
February	1-2-19-20-23-24-28-29	8-9-10-11-15-16	11	5-6-7-13-14-17-18
March	22-23-27-28	7-8-9-10-13-14-17-18	9-10-17-18	5-11-12-15-16
April	3-18-19-23-24-30	4-5-6-10-14	5-6-14	7-8-12-16-17
May	1-2-20-21-28-29-30-31	7-11-12-15-16	11-12	4-5-9-10-13-14
June	17-18-24-25-26-27	3-4-7-8-12-13	7-8	2-5-6-9-10-14-15
July	21-22-23-24-28-29	1-5-9-10-14	5-14	3-7-11-12
August	18-19-20-21-24-25	1-2-5-6-10-11-29	1-2-10-11-29	3-4-8-9-13-30-31
September	14-15-16-17-21-25	2-6-7-12-29-30	6-7	1-4-5-9-10-11-12-27-28
October	13-14-18-19-22-23	4-5-11-27-31	4-5-31	1-2-6-7-8-9-10-29
November	14-15-18-19-23-24	1-7-8-9-10-27-28	1-9-10-27-28	2-3-4-5-6-25-26-30
December	12-16-20-21	5-6-7-8-25-26	7-8-25-26	1-2-3-9-28-29-30-31

LUCKY NUMBERS
FOR LIBRA: 1996

Lucky numbers and astrology can be linked through the movements of the Moon. Each phase of the thirteen Moon cycles vibrates with a sequence of numbers for your Sign of the Zodiac over the course of the year. Using your lucky numbers is a fun system that connects you with tradition.

New Moon	First Quarter	Full Moon	Last Quarter
Dec. 21 ('95)	Dec. 28 ('95)	Jan. 5	Jan. 13
4 3 9 5	5 1 0 7	9 2 4 8	0 1 6 4
Jan. 20	Jan. 27	Feb. 4	Feb. 12
3 8 9 5	6 3 4 7	3 9 4 6	6 2 9 8
Feb. 18	Feb. 25	March 5	March 12
5 8 4 9	6 7 1 3	5 7 9 5	5 3 2 8
March 19	March 26	April 3	April 10
4 6 2 8	9 3 5 9	0 2 7 5	5 4 1 6
April 17	April 25	May 3	May 10
2 8 5 6	9 2 6 8	2 4 2 0	1 7 3 8
May 17	May 25	June 1	June 8
5 6 5 8	1 5 7 3	7 1 9 6	6 2 7 4
June 15	June 24	June 30	July 7
5 8 5 1	0 2 4 9	5 6 3 8	8 4 1 2
July 15	July 23	July 30	August 6
2 5 7 2	1 3 8 6	4 2 7 3	3 9 1 4
August 14	August 21	August 28	Sept. 4
6 0 1 3	8 3 1 9	1 2 7 4	4 5 8 0
Sept. 12	Sept. 20	Sept. 26	Oct. 4
1 5 7 3	1 9 1 7	6 8 5 6	6 9 2 0
Oct. 12	Oct. 19	Oct. 26	Nov. 3
0 8 4 2	1 7 1 6	2 8 9 3	3 5 9 2
Nov. 10	Nov. 17	Nov. 24	Dec. 3
2 7 5 4	1 6 9 5	8 3 6 8	8 3 5 0
Dec. 10	Dec. 17	Dec. 24	Jan. 2 ('97)
1 8 7 4	9 5 1 7	9 2 4 0	8 1 6 4

FREE CHOICE AND
THE VALUE OF PREDICTIONS

Now that you've had a chance to become familiar with
some basic astrological principles, it's time to turn our
attention to the matter of predictions. That was our original question after all: Can astrology peer into the
future? Well, astrological prognostication is an awe-in-
spiring art and requires deep philosophical consideration before it is to be undertaken. Not only are there
many grids that must be laid one upon the other before
such predictions can be made, but there are ethical issues that plague every student of the stars. How much
can you really see? How much should you tell? What is
the difference between valuable data and negative or
harmful programing?

If an astrologer tells you only the good things, you'll
have little confidence in the analysis when you are passing through crisis. On the other hand, if the astrologer is
a prophet of doom who can see nothing but the dark
clouds on the horizon, you will eventually have to reject
astrology because you will come to associate it with the
bad luck in your life.

Astrology itself is beyond any practitioner's capacity
to grasp it all. Unrealistic utopianism or gloomy de-
terminism reflect not the truth of astrology but the truth
of the astrologer interpreting what he sees. In order to
solve problems and make accurate predictions, you have
to be *able* to look on the dark side of things without
dwelling there. You have to be able to take a look at *all*
the possibilities, all the possible meanings of a certain
planetary influence without jumping to premature conclusions. Objective scanning and assessment take much
practice and great skill.

No matter how skilled the astrologer is, he cannot assume the responsibility for your life. Only you can take
that responsibility as your life unfolds. In a way, the

predictions of this book are glancing ahead up the road, much the way a road map can indicate turns up ahead this way or that. You, however, are still driving the car.

What then is a horoscope? If it is a picture of you at your moment of birth, are you then frozen forever in time and space, unable to budge or deviate from the harsh, unyielding declarations of the stars? Not at all.

The universe is always in motion. Each moment follows the moment before it. As the present is the result of all past choices and action, so the future is the result of today's choices. But if we can go to a planetary calendar and see where planets will be located two years from now, then how can individual free choice exist? This is a question that has haunted authors and philosophers since the first thinkers recorded their thoughts. In the end, of course, we must all reason things out for ourselves and come to our own conclusions. It is easy to be impressed or influenced by people who seem to know a lot more than we do, but in reality we must all find codes of beliefs with which we are the most comfortable.

But if we can stretch our imaginations up, up above the line of time as it exists from one point to another, we can almost see past, present and future, all together. We can almost feel this vibrant thread of creative free choice that pushes forward at every moment, actually causing the future to happen! Free will, that force that changes the entire course of a stream, exists within the substance of the stream of Mind itself. Past, present and future are mere stepping-stones across that great current.

Our lives continue a thread of an intelligent mind that existed before we were born and will exist after we die. It is like an endless relay race. At birth we pick up a torch and carry it, lighting the way through the darkness our whole lives with that miraculous light of consciousness of immortality, then we pass it on to others when we die. What we call the *unconscious* may be part of this great stream of Mind, which learns and shares experiences with everything that has ever lived or will ever live on this world or any other.

Yet we all come to Earth with different family circumstances, backgrounds and characteristics. We all come to life with different planetary configurations. Indeed each person *is* different, yet we are all the same. We have different tasks or responsibilities or life styles, but underneath we share a common current—the powerful stream of human intelligence. Each of us has different sets of circumstances to deal with because of the choices he or she has made in the past. We all possess different assets and have different resources to fall back on, weaknesses to strengthen and sides of our nature to transform. We are all what we are now because of what we were before. The present is the sum of the past. And we will be what we will be in the future because of what we are now. It's as simple as that.

It is foolish to pretend that there are no specific boundaries or limitations to any of our particular lives. Family background, racial, cultural or religious indoctrinations, physical characteristics, these are all inescapable facts of our being that must be incorporated and accepted into our maturing mind. But each person possesses the capacity for breakthrough, forgiveness and total transformation. It has taken millions of years since people first began to walk upright. We cannot expect an overnight evolution to take place. There are many things about our personalities that are very much like our parents. Sometimes that thought makes us uncomfortable, but it's true.

It's also true that we are not our parents. You are *you*, just you, and nobody else but you. That's one of the wondrous aspects of astrology. The levels on which each planetary configuration works out will vary from individual to individual. Often an aspect of selfishness will be manifested in one person, yet in another it may appear as sacrifice and kindness.

Development is inevitable in human consciousness. But the direction of that development is not. As plants will bend toward the light as they grow, so there is the possibility for the human mind to grow toward the light of integrity and truth. The Age of Aquarius that everyone is talking about must first take place within each man's mind and heart. An era of peace, freedom and brotherhood cannot be legislated by any government, no matter how liberal. It has to be a spontaneous flow of human spirit and fellowship. It will be a magnificent dawning on the globe of consciousness that reflects the joy of the human heart to be part of the great stream of intelligence and love. It must be generated by an enlightened, realistic humanity. There's no law that can put it into effect, no magic potion to drink that will make it all come true. It will be the result of all people's efforts to assume their personal and social responsibilities and carve out a new destiny for humankind.

As you read the predictions in this book, bear in mind that they have been calculated by means of planetary positions for whole groups of people. Thus their value lies in your ability to coordinate what you read with the nature of your life's circumstances at the present time. You have seen how many complex relationships must be analyzed in individual horoscopes before sensible accurate conclusions can be drawn. No matter what the indications, a person has his or her own life, own intelligence, basic native strength that must ultimately be the source of action and purpose. When you are living truthfully and in harmony with what you know is right, there are no forces, threats or obstacles that can defeat you.

With these predictions, read the overall pattern and see how rhythms begin to emerge. They are not caused by remote alien forces, millions of miles out in space. You and the planets are one. What you do, they do. What they do, you do. But can you change their course? No, but you cannot change many of your basic characteristics either. Still, within that already existing framework, you are the master. You can still differentiate between what is right for you and what is not. You can seize opportunities and act on them, you can create beauty and seek love. The purpose of looking ahead is not to scare yourself out of your wits. Look ahead to enlarge your perspective, enhance your overall view of the life *you* are developing. Difficult periods cause stress certainly, but at the same time they give you the chance to reassess your condition, restate and redefine exactly what is important to you, so you can cherish your life more. Joyous periods should be lived to the fullest with the happiness and exuberance that each person richly deserves.

We are not living to fulfill any destiny prerecorded long ago. We are not here as punishment for some past, forgotten sin. We are here because we choose to be here and take part in the vast evolving mystery we call human intelligence.

LIBRA
YEARLY FORECAST: 1996

Forecast for 1996 Concerning Business
Prospects, Financial Affairs, Health,
Travel, Employment, Love and Marriage
for Persons Born with the Sun
in the Zodiacal Sign of Libra,
September 23–October 22.

This promises to be an exciting year for those of you born under the influence of the Sun in the zodiacal sign of Libra, whose ruler is the loving planet Venus. The next twelve months are likely to present you with opportunities to learn to trust your instincts and to look after your own interests. The you who emerges will probably be more honest, forthright, and better equipped to make use of your creativity. As far as business and professional matters are concerned, this will be a time to become more independent and to stand your ground with colleagues and clients. Your interest in family matters may force you to compromise some of your long-term ambitions. You Libras are coming out of a long and possibly difficult financial phase. While there may have been ample reasons for being extremely careful about money in the past, you are approaching a time when it may be in your best interest to make more snap decisions and take more educated risks. In regard to health, your greatest danger, at least early in the year, can be stress due to overwork. This is also a time when you are likely to find the discipline and perseverance to develop reasonable diet and exercise programs and to stick to them. Travel is an area that is likely to bring changes

across the board. You Libras will have to make significant adjustments to how you get around, particularly
those short trips which you may have come to take for
granted. As far as job prospects are concerned, do not
be discouraged if the future looks bleak at first glance.
Stepped-up activity to find greener pastures can yield
more fruitful circumstances later on. You Libras take
your relationships seriously; and while family matters
may take up much of your attention early in the year,
some surprises can be coming your way. This can be
your year to fall in love at the drop of a hat. If you are
already married or in a committed relationship, 1996 is
likely to bring opportunities to work hard at resolving
long-standing conflicts.

Big changes can be in store for you Libra professionals in 1996. If you work in close partnership, this
is a time when your willingness to compromise and
smooth things over may be against your own best
interests. It may not be your nature to make snap decisions or be single-minded in reaching a goal. However, during the course of these entire twelve months you
can probably expect to lose out if you fall into old patterns of indecision or persist in following the path of
least resistance. While it is generally important and
part of your Libra charm to maintain friendly relations
with colleagues and clients, you may find yourselves
being more honest and straightforward in the manner
in which you conduct business. Those of you who have
recently started a family may find it difficult to work
toward the goals and ambitions that you once found so
meaningful. Whatever your individual circumstances,
this is a year when it will probably be of special importance to maintain a reasonable balance between your
professional life and your home life. Be careful not to
fall victim to ruthless agents who are more intent on
furthering their own careers than in representing you
fairly. If you feel cramped in your current offices, 1996

will be a good time to expand the space you have or move the whole operation to more suitable premises. Try not to base your square footage needs on unrealistic expectations about how much new business you are likely to attract.

Financially, you Libras are emerging from what may have felt like an extended testing period. Whatever lessons you have learned are sure to come in handy during 1996. As far as investments are concerned, again make sure that all those who are acting on your behalf are totally ethical. While it may be your style to play it safe in financial matters, do not be surprised if you find yourself taking more risks that has been your habit. An opportunity to make a big splash in the entertainment or high-tech industries may be difficult to resist. It may be wise to lie low on any risky ventures between January 8th and February 14th. Otherwise, balance is probably the best approach. Follow your instincts and gut feelings, but stay away from any investment opportunity which you even suspect to be less than ethical. Partnership issues are bound to enter into your financial life. April 20th to June 11th can be an especially critical time in this regard. If disagreements arise over how to handle long-term investments, try not to be the one who backs off in order to keep the peace. Real estate may be a lucrative investment, but have every inch of the property evaluated before you buy.

As far as health is concerned, you Libra professionals are cautioned not to fall victim to stress due to overwork. This may be particularly difficult to avoid between February 15th and March 23rd. Your body should be more than tuned in to its natural limits. Pay close attention to early symptoms of strain or stress, and you should be able to stay out of trouble. If an authoritarian employer or supervisor demands too much in the way of overtime, make it a point to assert your rights. That February to March period can also be an accident-prone time. You Libra do-it-yourselfers are advised not to take on projects that are beyond your level of skill or expertise. On the whole, 1996 will be a time when you may be more capable of sticking to diet and exercise programs than you have in the past. The healthy habits you develop between January 1st and April 6th should be able to stay with you throughout.

This year is likely to bring about shifts and developments that change the face of all forms of transportation. You Libras who are planning long-distance vacations abroad or in other parts of the country may have to be flexible about your destination and mode of transport. Make sure that the vacation sites you choose are not likely to be political or meteorological trouble spots. Try to schedule summer getaways after July 24th. However, it is short-distance travel that is more likely to be subject to big changes. Those of you who are accustomed to getting in the car for weekend spins in the countryside or driving out to visit relatives may have to find other means of getting where you want to go, or not going at all. At the same time, it is equally possible that trips you have been continually putting off will finally have to be made. Basically, as far as travel is concerned, the message is to be careful. Do not take driving for granted, and do not take any foolish chances while you are on the road.

Those of you who are unemployed or unhappy in your present jobs will see some positive activity during 1996. Job interviews tend to be intimidating for most people. Take that into consideration and try not to understate your experience or underestimate your abilities. If you find yourself put into a supervisory role, use the opportunity to develop your leadership qualities. Everyone may not love you at first, but you are probably going to be more effective if you stand firm on your standards and productivity expectations.

February 15th to March 23rd looks like a good cycle for job hunting. If you find yourself in the uncomfortable position of having to compete with a colleague or friend, it may be in the best interests of you both to sit down and have an honest talk. This probably will be no time to shy away from competition or sticky circumstances. If you go about it the right way, hurt feelings can be minimized if not eliminated. Try not to be discouraged if your search for a more ideal working situation does not materialize right away. It can be that efforts made during the first quarter of 1996 do not turn into actual employment until after April 6th.

Let's face it. You Libras, perhaps more than most people, love to be in love. If so, do not let the first couple of weeks of 1996 fool you. Big changes can be in store in the love department. Those of you who are single are likely to meet fascinating new people in the most unlikely circumstances. Do not be surprised if you find yourself attracted to people you may not have given any thought to in the past. Unconventional, creative types are especially likely to set your heart aflame over the course of the next twelve months. This may turn out to be disruptive to your friendships and group associations, but the excitement may be too much to resist. Try not to rush into any big romances between January 8th and February 14th. Concerning relationships of a more stable kind, those of you who have been involved for some time may decide to tie the knot in 1996. For those of you who have already been married or in committed relationships for some time, this will be an important year for working hard to resolve conflicts that have threatened your closeness. Remember that your most important relationship is with your own self. If you can keep that in mind and maintain a sense of independence and personal identity, your relationships with others are almost sure to benefit.

LIBRA
DAILY FORECAST: 1996

1st Week/January 1–7

Monday January 1st. This is likely to be a quiet start to the New Year. You may find that you are in a reflective mood. If domestic issues are weighing on your mind, be clear about your own wishes before you enter into any discussions with family members. If you are entertaining at home, go easy on the alcohol. Make sure that guests stay safely within the limit.

Tuesday the 2nd. This can be a good time for you Libra full-time students to settle down before the new term begins. If you are back at work, take the opportunity to put your desk in order before work starts piling up again. You Libra business people may want to devote part of the day to planning ahead for the coming months. Taking in a movie will make for a pleasant evening.

Wednesday the 3rd. You Libra job hunters are advised not to give in to feelings of despondency. Do not confine yourself to answering advertisements. If you ask around, you can hear of something through word of mouth. If you are at home, you may have to devote a lot of time to housework; putting the place back in order after festivities may take longer than you think.

Thursday the 4th. Resolve to take regular breaks from work this year. The occasional weekend away can do wonders for your health. A promotion is unlikely to be as straightforward as you were led to expect. You may be passed over this time, so guard against complacency. Socializing with colleagues this evening can be fun. But someone at home may object if you make too late a night of it.

Friday the 5th. If you are in the process of moving, this is likely to be a difficult day. Looking for a place to rent can consume more time than you have bargained for. Guard against taking the first thing that you see; patience is sure to pay off. This evening is unlikely to be favorable for entertaining at home. If you have friends visiting, stick to a restaurant you know is good.

Saturday the 6th. Try to accept the fact that an argument can be positive; clearing the air has got to be better than swallowing your feelings. A weekend job can be the answer to short-term financial problems, but the disruption it may cause to your home life may not make it worthwhile in the long run. If you are embarking on home improvements, guard against biting off more than you can chew.

Sunday the 7th. Young children can be a handful at present. Bad behavior is usually the result of boredom. Avoid staying at home all day. This can be a good day for sports of all kinds. But it is probably better to play for the fun of it rather than to win. Be cautious about airing your personal views in public; being outspoken can be mistaken for tactlessness by someone who does not know you well.

Weekly Summary

The year gets off to a running start, with the potential of putting you Libras in an expansive and optimistic mental and emotional state. The new cycle which begins on Wednesday will continue throughout the whole of the year. Those of you who were doing so much running around during the course of 1995 that you forgot which way was up should begin to feel much more settled. Look for a growing emphasis on the domestic side of life. Family problems that may have seemed too difficult to overcome may be resolved after all. If your current living situation is too cramped or unsuitable in another way, now is the time to make a better arrangement. That can mean expanding your home, or moving to another residence.

You Libras are known for having a great potential for seeing or making the world more beautiful. Whether this exists in you as a talent for painting, writing, or some other creative art, this should be a good time to make more room for self-expression in your life. The year actually begins with potentially positive changes from day one. You budding novelists may want to get down to business. Discover or rediscover the joy of indulging your creativity, even if that means writing a journal for your eyes only.

2nd Week/January 8–14

Monday the 8th. Someone you have set your heart on may not be responding in the way you hoped. Be patient and see what develops. Perhaps you have mistaken a friendship for love. A friend may come to you with problems in his or her own love life. Do not be tempted to say just what the person wants to hear; real friendship means being honest even if the truth is painful.

Tuesday the 9th. Try not to let paperwork claim too much of your time. If your car is acting up, this can be a good day for getting it into the garage. Do not rely on it until you do, as there is a risk of its breaking down. If you are at home, you will probably be in the mood for some peace and quiet. If you still have thank-you letters to write, do not put them off any longer.

Wednesday the 10th. Do not dwell on past mistakes; remind yourself that they are all part and parcel of the learning process. Your prospects for the future can be brighter than you think. If you put on some extra pounds over the festive period, this can be a good day for resolving on a diet and exercise program; there is a chance that you will stick to it.

Thursday the 11th. Trust your intuition; snap decisions are likely to be correct, and hunches can pay off. If you work in sales, this can be a good time for reviving old leads; a customer who did not buy last time may now be ready to do business. A direct and confident approach can open doors for you. Working with children can be rewarding; encourage their natural powers of imagination.

Friday the 12th. Meetings are likely to go well. Items on the agenda can be dealt with quickly and easily. This can be a propitious day for public speaking or sales presentations; avoid being too serious. This can be a favorable day for you Libra journalists. There is a chance of an exclusive just by being in the right place at the right time. A friendship may be showing signs of romance.

Saturday the 13th. You may feel as if you are spending a lot of time clearing up after other people. If you feel that you are being taken advantage of, say so. Avoid resorting to sarcasm. You are likely to get better results if you concentrate on stating your point of view clearly and concisely. Do not take unnecessary risks in sports. There is a risk of a minor injury.

Sunday the 14th. You may be able to pick up some genuine bargains for your home. Be prepared to haggle for items that are overpriced. You Libra parents may need to guard against losing your temper with your children. Constant squabbling can get on your nerves, but shouting probably will only make matters worse. This can be a testing day for a new romance. Keep a sense of proportion.

Weekly Summary

This is bound to be another dynamic week, full of a multitude of ups and downs. Those of you who have been trying to get back into the swing of things after the holidays may find that it will take more effort than anticipated. One of those potentially annoying cycles begins on Tuesday, which can make it difficult to accomplish simple, everyday tasks. If you expect and plan for breakdowns or delays in communication and transportation, you should be better prepared to keep things on an even keel. While this is a good time to make plans and sort out your goals, it is probably not at all suitable for coming to specific decisions or agreements. Contracts that are signed between now and the end of the month may come back for revision.

Another major cycle begins this week and can signal a whole new phase of life. Whereas everyone around you is on the verge of an important change, you Libras are most likely to experience it in your romantic lives or in your personal creativity. Those of you who are generally shy when it comes to matters of the heart may be ready to break through your insecurities. You are embarking on what will be an exciting journey where new people can enter your life at any turn.

3rd Week/January 15–21

Monday the 15th. Try to think of ways in which you can economize over the next couple of weeks. You Libra employees may be offered the chance to do some overtime. This may be the last thing you feel like doing, but the extra money will make it worthwhile. Someone close to you may be going through a difficult patch. Let the person know your support is there.

Tuesday the 16th. Avoid leaving important paperwork lying around; there is a risk of its going astray. If you are sending documents through the mail, it may be a wise move to use a special delivery service to be sure it reaches its destination safely. For you Libra parents, this can be a lucky time for finding a new babysitter, especially if recommended by a relative or neighbor.

Wednesday the 17th. Allow extra time for your journey to work this morning, especially if you have an important meeting lined up. There is a greater chance of delays on public transport, such as train cancellations or traffic jams. If you are parking in town, make sure that you do so legally; it is not worth running the risk of a ticket or even being towed away.

Thursday the 18th. This can be a good day for working from home. The fewer distractions you have, the more you will get done. You Libra office workers can find this a good time for reorganizing your work space. Later on, catch up with domestic tasks, such as cleaning or ironing. Make a point of sharing the evening meal with those you live with; a friend may drop by.

Friday the 19th. This can be a productive day for house hunting; make sure that you put in an offer right away on the place you want. At work, this is likely to be a low-key end to the week. If you are up against a deadline, you should find that you are able to meet it relatively easily. This evening can be good for entertaining at home; this can be cheaper than a night out.

Saturday the 20th. You will enjoy your free time more if you know that your chores are up to date. Guard against impulsive spending. Pay for things in cash; that way you can be more realistic. If you have small children with you, make sure that you keep them in sight at all times; they may wander off when your back is turned. A night out can result in a surprise romantic opportunity.

Sunday the 21st. Friction between you and another member of your family can come to a head. A long-standing disagreement needs to be resolved; so do not avoid the conflict, no matter how much you hate confrontation. If you have a high-pressure job during the week you may consider balancing this out with something relaxing, such as yoga or writing in a journal.

Weekly Summary

It is not often that so many changes happen so early in the year, but 1996 appears to be an exception. A short but important cycle begins on Monday which involves your very own ruling planet, Venus. This shift may make it easier than ever to organize the tasks and details of your daily life. Those of you who have been thinking about expanding your household by getting a dog, cat, or other animal may want to start making a move. Do not fail to consider adopting an abandoned animal that has found its way to the local shelter. An older pet who has already been trained can sometimes be easier than a fiesty puppy or kitten.

Another short but important cycle begins on Sunday which is likely to shed some light on your love life.

Those of you who are free and available are headed for what may be an exciting time as far as romance is concerned. If you have recently become independent of your family, you may be feeling enthusiastic about getting out and having fun. However, try to make use of your famous Libra sense of balance. Do not rush into what may turn out to be disruptive relationships.

4th Week/January 22–28

Monday the 22nd. Take extra care with written work, especially if someone is piling on the pressure. You are more likely to make mistakes if you allow yourself to be hurried. A personal letter that you were expecting may not turn up on time. If your telephone bill is already overdue, make sure that you pay it immediately to avoid the risk of being disconnected.

Tuesday the 23rd. A medical checkup can set your mind at rest about a minor health worry. For you Libra employees, this will be a day when you should not shy away from taking on extra responsibilities. Your willingness to put in extra time and effort is sure to be noticed. A request for promotion or a raise will probably be taken seriously; someone may value you more highly than you realize.

Wednesday the 24th. In your desire to please everyone, make sure that you don't agree to unreasonable requests. Social invitations are likely to be in abundance. Again, guard against making too many commitments. It is better to say no now rather than let someone down at the last moment. If you are married, this will be a good evening for time with your spouse.

Thursday the 25th. Listen carefully to your partner's ideas. Guard against sticking to outdated principles; be prepared to embrace new challenges. It is in your best interests to be meticulous in business dealings of all kinds now. Do not ignore the small print. Enter appointments or social invitations in your diary as soon as they are made. You may have a tendency to be absentminded.

Friday the 26th. Avoid being caught up in office politics; a certain individual may be painting a one-sided picture. There is probably nothing to be gained by trying to fight someone else's battle; it can prove to be a thankless task. Trust your gut instincts; if you feel that someone is lying, you probably are right. Do not take any information as gospel without checking it first.

Saturday the 27th. Make a point of relaxing this weekend. Gentle exercise, such as walking or swimming, can be ideal. The solution to a personal problem may be staring you in the face; give yourself time to think things through. You Libra parents of teenage children will be wise to be firm without laying down the law too strongly. Rebellion at this age is natural; ask yourself if you are being too strict.

Sunday the 28th. Therapy can be invaluable in helping you understand problems within your family circle. You may be able to heal a rift that has been a source of sadness. This can be a day of confidences. A loved one may want to discuss a personal matter with you. Being a good listener will probably be just as important as offering the benefit of your own experience.

Weekly Summary

Partnership issues, which are particularly important to you Libras, are likely to take the spotlight for much of this week. Relationships with professional colleagues are sure to flourish if you can be supportive of one another's bright ideas. Wednesday will be ideal for putting your heads together. Remember to keep your mind open. As for close encounters of the intimate variety, those of you who are free and available are advised to keep your eyes and heart open too. You may meet a most interesting person when you least expect it. If just the idea makes you feel insecure and tongue-tied, do what you can to lighten up.

They say that the whole universe is nothing but energy which can be used in positive or negative ways. Make sure the emotional energies flowing through you on Friday and the weekend do not throw you off kilter. One way to avoid feeling dark or moody is to have a nice long chat with an old friend. If that fails, paint or write your feelings. The main point is to let all those thoughts and feelings flow.

5th Week/January 29–February 4

Monday the 29th. A fresh start on a difficult piece of written work will pay dividends. Legal matters may be held up through errors or delays with paperwork. Avoid putting your signature to any document that you do not fully understand; seek expert advice if in doubt. A new romance can be in the cards, maybe with someone of a different ethnic origin. Language barriers can be overcome.

Tuesday the 30th. If your child is having problems at school, this can be a good time for a personal talk with the teacher. There is a good chance that you can come up with helpful ideas. Working with children can be challenging but tiring; you may wonder where they get their energy. Investments with overseas companies can prove to be lucrative. A gamble should pay off.

Wednesday the 31st. This may be a lucky day for finding a new job. Even if the position is not ideal, it can lead to other opportunities. Setting yourself achievable targets can be the key to success. If the pressure is off at the office, you may consider taking a potential customer out for lunch to establish a closer rapport. This evening can be low-key but enjoyable.

Thursday February 1st. If you are thinking of becoming self-employed, get expert advice on taxes and insurance. For you Libra employers, this can be a favorable time for introducing a bonus system for your staff. The extra incentive will do wonders for production. If you are applying for a better job, knowing your own worth can make the right impression.

Friday the 2nd. Avoid crossing swords with a superior. You are almost sure to come out the loser. Do not say anything that you do not want repeated. Concentrate on doing your own work to the best of your ability. A colleague may be willing to take a time-consuming project off your hands. Later, a sauna or steam bath can be just what you need to relax.

Saturday the 3rd. Make a point of replying to personal letters right away. If someone has got into the habit of letting you down at the last minute, feel free to object. A brother or sister may drop by. If either has small children, an offer to babysit for a few hours will probably be gratefully accepted. Keep a wary eye out for gate-crashers if you are having a party this evening.

Sunday the 4th. This is unlikely to be a good day for being cooped up inside with young children. Do not wait for others to make the move. Take the initiative to call around your circle of friends or family. Friction within a romantic relationship can come to a head.

Realize that you must allow partners the freedom to live their own lives as well as sharing in yours.

Weekly Summary

You hardworking Libras who have been driven around the bend by anything from postal delays to computer malfunctions to missed trains and lost messages can begin to breathe a sigh of relief. That devilish and irritating cycle which strikes at least two times a year is officially over on Tuesday. Although communications and short-distance travel may take a bit longer to completely stabilize, you should be able to sign contracts and make major purchases without too much anxiety that you have made the wrong decision.

Professional concerns are likely to take center stage by Wednesday. Those of you who are hoping to make significant advances in your careers can receive encouraging news on Thursday. However, do not count your chickens before they are hatched. If you do, a whole new series of problems can unfold, especially if family members are already feeling cheated by all the time you spend away from home. Probably nobody knows as well as you Libras do that life is a balancing act. When conflicts arise between your professional life and your home life, sit down and see what specific steps you can take to find some middle ground.

6th Week/February 5–11

Monday the 5th. If you are starting a new job, do not panic if you do not pick up some things right away. Learning is a gradual process. If you are unattached, you may have an unknown admirer, perhaps someone you have met through work. Look out for the signs. He or she may be waiting for some encouragement.

Try not to worry about a lost object; there is a good chance that it will turn up.

Tuesday the 6th. This should be an excellent day for moving your residence or relocating your business premises. The upheaval is likely to be far less trouble than expected. Take personal responsibility for valuable objects. This can be a favorable time for investing in antiques or works of art. A grandparent may be generous with money or passing on family heirlooms.

Wednesday the 7th. Pay extra attention to small details. If you need help, do not be too proud to ask for it. A colleague should be only too willing to lend a hand. A loved one's health may be giving you cause for concern; but there can be a reluctance to seek a medical opinion. You may have to intervene even at the cost of an argument; stress that you have the best interests of the person at heart.

Thursday the 8th. Someone may be relying on you more than you realize. Business meetings need to be tackled with more sensitivity than usual. You should be able to bring a certain individual around to your way of thinking if you can be patient. For you Libra salespeople, this can be a favorable day for working on the telephone; tying up loose ends in this way can save you a lot of valuable time.

Friday the 9th. If your work calls upon your artistic or creative skills, this is likely to be a productive day; inspiration can strike just when you need it most. Praise from a superior can make you feel valued. This can be a favorable day for giving yourself a new look. You can afford to be adventurous with your appearance. A first date is almost sure to be a success.

Saturday the 10th. Keep a close hold on your wallet. There is a risk of being pickpocketed or of absentmindedness. This can be a good time for investing in labor-saving devices for the kitchen, for instance, a food processor or a microwave oven. You married Libras may have an argument over your children; but this should be quickly resolved. Enjoy a romantic dinner with your partner.

Sunday the 11th. The behavior of loved ones can leave you feeling confused or puzzled; this may be deliberate secretiveness on their part. Respect their privacy. They are sure to confide in you when they are ready. This can be a good time for turning your hand to creative writing. Writing things down is often the way to make sense of something. This evening lends itself to relaxing at home.

Weekly Summary

A pleasant new cycle begins this week. It can bring a welcome boost to all your relationships, whether they be personal or professional. Those of you who have been suffering from feeling critical of or criticized by your partners should be able to find ways of making peace without having to make too many sacrifices. If you have been negotiating a legal settlement or contract, you should be able to get the details out of the way and start to wrap things up. If things do not work out to your mutual advantage, you may have yourself to blame. Try not to let your emotional sensitivity get the better of you. You may be feeling threatened or wounded by conflicts that exist only in your imagination. If you are willing to talk over your misgivings, you are almost sure to clear things up.

Keep a tight hold on your wallet over the weekend. The urge to splurge may be hard to resist. If you feel you absolutely must treat yourself to something beautiful, steer yourself into shops that have household furnishings that are functional as well as aesthetic. The latest entertainment gadgets are best avoided now.

7th Week/February 12–18

Monday the 12th. A meeting with an accountant or financial adviser may provide you with some helpful tips on saving taxes. Your cash-flow situation should be healthy at the moment. Keep it that way by asking for a deposit when taking on new work. Buying a secondhand car can be a risky business. Get an expert's opinion before you part with your cash.

Tuesday the 13th. Administrative matters can be time consuming; you may have to put in some overtime if you want to bring everything up to date. Face-to-face business dealings can be more productive than working on the telephone. Do not be complacent about securing new business. If you are buying from a catalogue, make sure you can return unwanted goods.

Wednesday the 14th. If you have lost the habit of writing letters, this can be a good time for reviving it. A Valentine card or a love letter is often more meaningful than a phone call. Looking after children can be fun if you enter into the spirit of their games. If you are seeking to widen your social circle, take up a new hobby. This way you are sure to meet people with whom you have something in common.

Thursday the 15th. Do-it-yourself jobs may be easier to tackle than you realize. Make a point of brightening up your place of work. Some fresh flowers or plants can make all the difference. A colleague who is clearly not in a good mood can soon be won over with some cheerfulness on your part. In this way you should be able to hearten the person rather than sinking into the same mood yourself.

Friday the 16th. Lunch with a friend can be an entertaining occasion; you both are likely to be in the mood for a heart-to-heart talk. You single Libras who are on the threshold of a new romance may need to guard against building up your hopes too high. Remind yourself that if you idealize someone, you are almost sure to be disappointed when expectations are not met.

Saturday the 17th. The company of close friends or loved ones can be a real tonic. Laughter is the best medicine. A new romance can bring color to your life; let your partner know just how much he or she is appreciated. If you are a single parent, this can be a good time for introducing a new partner to your children; they should take to one another easily. This is a good evening for live music of all kinds.

Sunday the 18th. Neither fitness nor skills are achieved overnight. Do not push yourself. If a social occasion proves to be boring, make your excuses and leave. Be sensible with your diet. You are more likely to feel the ill effects of too much alcohol or rich food. This can be a favorable time for giving up something that is bad for you, such as coffee or junk food.

Weekly Summary

You Libras who work in office jobs may find it difficult to concentrate this week. If someone is being an exceptionally hard taskmaster, it may be good to remind him or her what happens to Jack when life is all work and no play. A midweek staff lunch at a restaurant may evoke more loyalty and productivity than a hard-line approach. You can probably expect people to buckle down and take their work more seriously after Thursday anyway. That is when a new cycle is likely to make everyone strive to be efficient.

Get ready for an early start to what promises to be an exciting weekend. An out-of-the-blue invitation can do wonders to raise your spirit. If one is not forthcoming, feel free to get on the phone and be bold about inviting someone out yourself. Spontaneous get-togethers are bound to be fun. And remember, those of you who are in long-term relationships are not immune to falling in love all over again with one another. But don't wait until the last minute to set aside time for romance.

8th Week/February 19–25

Monday the 19th. Try not to take tactless remarks to heart. While it is natural to want others to think well of you, realize that that is not always possible or meaningful. Avoid being drawn into pointless arguments where you might say things that you will regret later. Hard work will pay dividends; determination to succeed should get you the results that you deserve.

Tuesday the 20th. A jog or a swim can be the way to revitalize yourself. You Libra employees can have a tough day in front of you. You may have to make key decisions if a superior is not available. Just use your common sense. A health problem may not be responding to conventional treatment. You may decide to see a practitioner of alternative medicine.

Wednesday the 21st. At work, make sure the right hand knows what the left hand is doing. This can be a lucky day for you Libras who are being interviewed for a job; there is a chance of an immediate rapport with your potential employer. Your enthusiasm can count for just as much as the experience or qualifications you have to offer. A surprise telephone call can result in a fun night out.

Thursday the 22nd. Do not allow yourself to be sweet-talked into buying things you do not really want. You unattached Libras may be nursing a secret crush. Find out more about the person before you stick your neck out. Do not be tempted to cover up mistakes; even a white lie can be found out. Others are likely to be forgiving if you are honest about your own shortcomings.

Friday the 23rd. This can be a demanding end to the working week. It may be hard to hold onto your professional attitude. If you have money to invest, this can be a good time for shopping around for the best deals. A financial adviser can come up with some valuable tips, but do not allow anyone else to make up your mind for you. Guard against being too possessive.

Saturday the 24th. If you feel the need for solitude, do not be afraid to say so. Your loved ones will be more understanding than anticipated. Remind yourself that everyone needs time alone occasionally. This evening can be perfect for being with old friends or someone else who is important to you. You may feel the need to discuss matters of an intensely personal nature.

Sunday the 25th. You should get the most out of the day if you plan an outing. A short train or car journey to visit friends can be fun. If you are going into town, you may decide to visit an art gallery or a museum. All activities that are educational should be worthwhile. You Libra full-time students may have to devote a part of the day to studies. Set realistic targets.

Weekly Summary

A short but important cycle gets underway this week. It can present a good opportunity to confront any health concerns that have been worrying you. Those of you who have been burning the candle at both ends should realize that stress and overwork are not trivial matters. If you move your brain cells more than any other part of your body, it is probably high time to get into some kind of exercise program. Movement can make all the difference in the world for those of you who lead sedentary life-styles.

By midweek, partnership issues will begin to take more of your attention. Those of you who work in collaboration with someone else should feel free to share your creative thoughts. This is no time to hold back because you are afraid of making a fool of yourself.

Those of you who work in any of the creative arts are probably not in need of any reminders about how difficult it can be to earn a living at it. It may be inevitable that you have to get a so-called regular job in order to pay your household expenses. However, it can be a mistake to neglect your creative side.

9th Week/February 26–March 3

Monday the 26th. This can be a good time for dealing with companies overseas. Long-distance travel, either for leisure or business purposes, should be without complications. A fellow passenger may prove to be entertaining company. If you are ready for an intellectual challenge, this can be a good time for signing up for an evening class, perhaps to learn a new language.

Tuesday the 27th. Make sure you have work to do or a good book to read if you are traveling by train or air.

There is a likelihood of delays. You Libra parents who have children in higher education may be feeling the pinch financially. This will not go on forever. Book tickets now for interesting upcoming cultural events.

Wednesday the 28th. You Libra professionals may consider spending more on your advertising or public relations campaigns. Employing an outside agency will be money well spent. If you are under a lot of pressure at work, guard against letting your personal life suffer; try to keep a sense of perspective. For instance, try to keep overtime at a realistic level.

Thursday the 29th. If you are bored with your job, now is the time to start looking for something more challenging. Guard against letting yourself sink into apathy. If a business appointment is canceled at the last minute, reschedule it as soon as possible. You single Libras should think carefully about getting involved with someone from work; mixing business with pleasure is not always a successful recipe.

Friday March 1st. Guard against delegating too many tasks; the key to success may lie in checking details for yourself. Meetings can go on longer than expected; reaching a consensus is unlikely to be straightforward. Business deals struck over the telephone need to be confirmed in writing. This evening can be good for going out with friends or group meetings.

Saturday the 2nd. You are likely to be in a sociable mood now. If you have not made any plans for this evening, you may consider an impromptu party at home; several friends may also be at loose ends. If you prefer something more intimate, invite a few close friends over for dinner. This can be an excellent time for picking up the pieces of your social life.

Sunday the 3rd. People may be making unreasonable demands on your time. If they are lonely, it does not mean that you have to fill the gap. Not allowing yourself to be put upon is better than feeling resentful. This afternoon can be good for going out to visit friends or just to the park. Do not allow a squabble with your partner to depress you; remind yourself of the good points of your love.

Weekly Summary

You forward-thinking Libras are advised to set aside some time this week to consider your long-term plans and dreams. There is a danger of losing sight of the forest for the trees. Try to remember the promises you may have made to yourself at the beginning of the year. There is no time like the present to make them realities. This can mean looking into further education, either for your own pleasure or to prepare for a new career. If you have always wanted to travel, why not see if there is a way to mix business with pleasure? A fact-finding mission to a potential foreign market will make solid professional sense. As far as your professional aspirations are concerned, you probably will be wise to expect conflicts with family members or partners. Make it a point to consider their needs lest you find yourself facing some tough times.

Those of you who are involved in humanitarian or political groups are advised to think before acting this week. Making irresponsible or self-serving statements to the media can tarnish the image of your group.

10th Week/March 4–10

Monday the 4th. A colleague's ineptitude may be driving you mad. Try to find a way of giving advice without interfering. Being critical will make matters worse. If you are at home at present and have some free time, clear out a hidden corner; throw out old junk and donate unwanted items to a charity. You may hear from an old flame. It will be fun to meet somewhere.

Tuesday the 5th. If you are feeling that life is all work and no play, make a point of looking up old friends or arranging a night out. This can be a favorable time for finishing a project that has been dragging on so that you can sink your teeth into something more interesting. A loved one who is in need will probably appreciate a visit. Put your worries aside to give cheer.

Wednesday the 6th. This should be a good day for furthering your aims and ambitions. Have the confidence to apply for a better job or a higher position; you may find that the competition is not as stiff as you expect. If you know that you are underpaid for what you do, now is the time to request a pay raise. Knowing your own worth can make a superior take you seriously.

Thursday the 7th. If you want something done well, do it yourself. Other people may be quick to make promises that they cannot honor. If you go out on a job interview, dress conventionally; do not underestimate the importance of first impressions. This is unlikely to be a good day for drastic changes to your appearance. Stick to a hairdresser you trust.

Friday the 8th. If you are planning to buy your first home, now is the time to work out the costs involved. Thus you can avoid overstretching yourself. This should be an excellent day for you Libras who make your living from writing. A children's story may be sold for a healthy price. If you are an aspiring singer or actor, this day your luck can turn for the better.

Saturday the 9th. You Libras who are unattached may be asked out by someone you have admired. Nerves can make you tongue-tied at first. Concentrate on finding out more about the other person. Showing a genuine interest is often the way to break the ice. You may be asked to give a home to a puppy or kitten; think carefully about the responsibilities involved.

Sunday the 10th. Check pockets of clothes before you put them in the washing machine; they may contain a forgotten letter. Getting out to the countryside can be revitalizing. If you have a joint bank account with your partner, you may need to assess your financial situation. If you can keep track of what each other is spending, you should be able to avoid arguments.

Weekly Summary

An important planetary event on Tuesday is likely to influence the internal climate of the whole week. Those of you who work with others may want to keep a low profile, especially on Monday and Tuesday. If it is possible to find a quiet corner where you can work on your own, by all means go for it. You may not realize how much stress there is in the atmosphere until somebody blows up. Try not to add to the problem by poisoning the air with unspoken complaints or resentments. Use your famous Libra charm to find diplomatic ways of making your needs known. Bottling them up probably will not do anybody any good.

You are likely to feel more confident about your current situation by the time Wednesday rolls around. However, be careful not to step on other people's toes. Those of you who are self-employed or working on a project independently can become so single-minded that you neglect other areas of your life.

If your home is far from the dream house you are longing for, you may be able to remedy the situation earlier than you think. Developing some basic do-it-yourself skills will come in very handy right now.

11th Week/March 11–17

Monday the 11th. If a superior passes on work without clear instructions, making guesses can end up wasting more time. If you are working on a word processor, don't forget to back up your work; there is a risk of losing it. An argument with a brother or sister can leave you stewing. Guard against bearing a grudge. If you are in the wrong, apologize. If you are owed an apology, ask for it.

Tuesday the 12th. This can be a favorable time for buying a personal organizer to keep track of special dates. If work is piling up, it may be that you are mismanaging your time. Try to improve your efficiency. For instance, you should adopt the habit of making a list of tasks in order of priority and ticking them off as you go. Your telephone bill may be higher than usual.

Wednesday the 13th. You Libras are usually gifted when it comes to making your home a beautiful place. Put this talent to use now by splashing out on fresh flowers or other adornments. Joint finances should be healthy at the moment; your partner may announce news of a raise or a larger bonus than expected. A formal dinner party should prove to be splendid.

Thursday the 14th. Someone with whom you work closely may be too preoccupied with personal matters to get things done effectively. Make an extra effort to be tolerant. A loved one may want to do his or her own thing this evening; realize that there is no need to live in each other's pockets when it comes to your social life. This can be a good evening for catching up with routine jobs at home.

Friday the 15th. Be prepared to be flexible with your schedule. An unexpected promotion at your place of work can be the cause of some discontent; try not to get involved in gossip, which is probably based on jealousy. A child may be in need of extra love and attention. A social occasion with your colleagues can be fun this evening; you can get to know someone better.

Saturday the 16th. A love affair that is still in the early stages can benefit from spending some time together. Remind yourself that you cannot hope to get to know someone if you are continually surrounded by friends or family. You may want to pass up a party invitation this evening in favor of a night at home, either alone or in the company of a loved one.

Sunday the 17th. If you are starting a fitness program, guard against overdoing it. Pushing yourself too hard will result in exhaustion or even an injury. Remember that you are what you eat; this can be a good time for casting a critical eye over your diet. You might decide to try vitamin or mineral supplements for extra vitality, especially if you drink or smoke.

Weekly Summary

Presentations and written assignments can leave you bogged down in paperwork during the early part of the week. If it looks as though you cannot meet your deadline, it is probably better to get it postponed, rather than to try to fudge your way through it with sloppy work.

Those of you who are in the market for real estate may have a bit of welcome news this week. If you are considering the purchase of a property for investment purposes, make sure you get a comprehensive survey done of everything from the foundation to the plumbing and the roof. Leave ample funds in your budget for repairs that may have to be made in the future. Do not let agents who are eager to make a sale pull the wool over your eyes.

Friday and Saturday look like good bets for entertaining. Those of you with children in your care may be shocked at how expensive a day out can be. Try to find alternatives by making good use of your imagination. Playing pretend games together will not only be fun, it will also be revealing about what your child is thinking and feeling.

12th Week/March 18–24

Monday the 18th. You Libras who are starting a new job this morning can find yourselves being thrown in at the deep end. Do not be afraid to ask questions, even if others seem to be busy. It is your colleagues' duty to make time for you. This can be a favorable day for finishing off written work. If you are unemployed, just asking around can produce results quickly.

Tuesday the 19th. This can be a propitious day for new business ventures of all kinds. A new promotion should take off better than you hope. If you have an ongoing health problem, this can be an excellent time for trying new practitioners maybe in the field of alternative medicine. They may succeed where others have failed. A new liaison can blossom into romance.

Wednesday the 20th. Think twice before going into business with a partner. If you are going through the unhappy process of divorce, this is a day when you may not be able to avoid some conflict with your partner. While it is important not to lose out financially, do not attach too much importance to shared material goods. Your emotional well-being is more important.

Thursday the 21st. Realize that you cannot be all things to all people. This is a day when you should put your own work at the top of your list of priorities; other people's problems can wait. You Libras who are unattached may have had an infatuation with someone, but there is a chance that the person will topple from his or her pedestal. Remind yourself that nobody is perfect.

Friday the 22nd. This can be a favorable time for taking a look at your long-term financial position. You should consider investing in an endowment policy. If you do not have a pension plan through your work, this can be a good time for taking out one of your own. Your other insurance needs may need to be updated to cover the contents of your home.

Saturday the 23rd. This can be a good day for visiting other members of your family who live nearby. An older relative may be able to fill a gap in your early life history. Talking about your childhood can bring back a mixed bag of memories. It may be tempting to resort to sarcasm in an argument with a loved one; but open discussion is more important than trying to score points.

Sunday the 24th. The summer vacation may be up for discussion. Browse through some travel brochures. You may consider going to a country that you have not visited before. Visiting an art exhibit or a museum can be a pleasant way to spend the afternoon. If you are in the mood for staying at home, you may want to rent a good movie from the video shop.

Weekly Summary

This can turn out to be an important week for you Libras, especially in the area of your partnerships and personal relationships. Those of you who have been insecure about sharing your feelings may find yourselves ready to cast your fate to the wind. This is a time when you are much more likely to feel better by speaking your mind than by trying to let things go when you know you really cannot. Your Libra charm, which may have relied heavily on small talk in the past, will probably have to find more honest and meaningful ways of making contact. While that may seem scary at first, the accompanying growth of your personal integrity should be an effective motivator.

Money matters may be uppermost in your mind by late on Thursday. This is probably no time to speculate in the stock market, or to take any other financial gambles, for that matter. Friday looks much more solid for making investment decisions. Your long-term security needs to be taken seriously. Conservative investments may be a better bet in the long run. Make a painstaking analysis of a company's past performance rather than relying on hunches.

13th Week/March 25–31

Monday the 25th. This can be a propitious day for business dealings with overseas contacts. You may decide to arrange long-distance business trips to cement a promising working relationship. You Libra employers who are in need of extra staff may consider taking on young people through a government training program. A new romance can develop if you take the plunge.

Tuesday the 26th. If you have been made a scapegoat, it is up to you to stand up for yourself. Do not allow yourself to be intimidated by people who are abusing their power. If you do not object to such treatment now, you will run the risk of it happening again. A family argument may be caused by the generation gap. Make an extra effort to see the situation from the other person's point of view.

Wednesday the 27th. Do not be seduced into a business project just because of someone else's enthusiasm. Check out the facts. A chance for promotion can come your way. But the extra salary needs to be weighed carefully against your domestic commitments; your partner may feel that he or she is taking second place to your professional life.

Thursday the 28th. Do not let outstanding invoices remain unpaid. This can be a favorable time for acting on advice from your lawyer. If you are on the short list for a new job, be prepared to be sent for a medical exam. Make the most of the opportunity for a thorough checkup. Do not let a doctor brush you off with vague explanations; it is your body and you have a right to full answers.

Friday the 29th. Bouncing ideas off a colleague can be useful. This is a day when it probably is best not to take sole responsibility for decisions at work; other people may wish to have their opinions taken into account. Later in the day, put your problems out of your head and concentrate on enjoying yourself. You unattached Libras can meet somebody new through a mutual acquaintance.

Saturday the 30th. You may have to curtail social activities until your financial situation takes a turn for the better. This is unlikely to be a favorable time for borrowing from friends. Being in debt to someone will put an uncomfortable strain on your relationship. If your partner prefers to spend time with personal friends, try not to feel left out or sulky. Learn to enjoy your own company.

Sunday the 31st. Make a point of finding time to relax. A worn-out romance may need to be laid to rest once and for all. You may have to accept the fact that a clean break is the best answer for you both. Talking through a personal problem with a loved one can be reassuring. But avoid collecting opinions from other people; your own feelings are what really count.

Weekly Summary

You hardworking Libra professionals may be reminded of the down side of all your aspirations and success. They say it is lonely at the top; if that rings a bell with you, make a special effort to keep your life more balanced. It is important to acknowledge and devote time to your need to find your niche and make your mark; but if your personal life suffers too much in the process, it may be time to slow down and devise a more reasonable strategy. All the financial rewards in the world cannot fulfill your need for closeness and intimacy.

Those of you who are looking for ways to expand your social circle may want to explore groups and small societies in your area. Check out the local newspaper to see if any special events listings catch your interest. Like-minded people who share the same ideals and philosophy can add an important new dimension to your life. However, it will probably take some initiative on your part to find them. Friday looks ideal for making new contacts. Avoid groups that seem to have a hidden agenda or ulterior motive in attracting new members.

14th Week/April 1–7

Monday April 1st. This morning's mail may include news from friends or members of your family who have been out of touch for a long time. A long-standing feud needs to be resolved; realize that there is nothing to be gained from holding onto bad feelings that belong in the past. Your offer to bury the hatchet is almost sure to be accepted with great relief.

Tuesday the 2nd. Meetings of a confidential nature should be scheduled before lunch. Do not expect all decisions to meet with your approval. Bide your time; fresh information can emerge to throw a whole new light on the matter. Later hours in the day can be good for dealing with correspondence and administration of all kinds. Romance can come when you least expect it.

Wednesday the 3rd. You Libras will often go to great lengths to avoid confrontation, but you may just have to accept that taking the line of least resistance is not always possible. If you are feeling depressed, realize that this may be the result of keeping anger locked up inside you. It may be wise to remind yourself that the only person who suffers from this sort of denial is you.

Thursday the 4th. Some of you will be busy preparing for Passover. Glowing accounts of people's work history may not be as faultless as they would have you believe. If you are interested in buying an old property, pay for an independent survey; that way you know exactly what you are up against regarding renovation costs. Partners can be in a difficult mood this evening.

Friday the 5th. Those of you who are unemployed may want to check into job training programs. If you are a single parent, you may be entitled to more assistance than you realize. Do not turn down help from a loved one out of pride; you can always repay a loan when times are easier. If you have had a heavy week you may be weary of people. A night in will appeal.

Saturday the 6th. Guard against wasting money. If you hunt around, there is a good chance that you will find the same items at much cheaper prices. If you are traveling a long distance by car, make sure that you check oil, gas, and water before you set out. If you are not already a member of an automobile association, it will be a wise move to join one now.

Sunday the 7th. You Libras who have strong religious beliefs will want to attend a church service this Easter morning. The lesson may be particularly meaningful for you. If you are traveling by public transport, it may be a wise move to allow more time than usual for your journey. Your partner can make a point of showing how much he or she appreciates you.

Weekly Summary

Two major planetary shifts occur during the course of this week. The first occurs on Wednesday and can add a dynamic new dimension to your life. Venus, which is the ruler of your Sun sign Libra, moves out of what may have been a somewhat difficult position. Those of you who have felt tortured by a relationship that has had no possibility of going anywhere will feel ready to start sprouting your wings. Exploration is the name of the game for this next cycle. Seek out people from different countries, cultures, and backgrounds who can expand your personal horizons.

The next change, occuring on Sunday, may have more far-reaching implications. Those of you who have been haggling over the details of a new partnership or any other kind of agreement can finally find yourselves signing on the bottom line. Although you may feel more fearful or cautious about entering into collaborative projects, the ones that meet your high standards are quite likely to be long lasting. An older or more experienced person may come onto the scene, helping you to become more mature in your approach to dealing with others.

15th Week/April 8–14

Monday the 8th. Sharing a laugh can do wonders to improve the atmosphere at work. This can be a favorable time for signing up with an employment agency; it may be able to keep you in work for at least the immediate future. A temporary post can develop into a permanent one once someone realizes how capable you are. Brush up your computer skills.

Tuesday the 9th. There is probably no point in trying to force decisions at the moment. Some off-the-record information can be useful. This can be a good time for keeping tabs on your business rivals; forewarned can be forearmed. Problems within a personal relationship may appear insurmountable; do not give up too soon.

Wednesday the 10th. You Libra business people will find this an unfavorable day for gambles, especially ones that involve large amounts of money. You cannot afford to trust to luck; your gut instincts may not be as reliable as usual. If you are placing bets on sports events of any kind, your best policy now is moderation. Guard against nagging your partner this evening.

Thursday the 11th. Pushing forward innovative ideas at work may not be as easy as you imagine. There is always someone who prefers to stick to the tried and trusted. If you present your proposals carefully, you may eventually be able to win someone over to your way of thinking. Avoid putting your signature to any documents that you do not fully understand.

Friday the 12th. Notice how your good humor rubs off on those around you. It should be gratifying to find yourself high in the popularity stakes. For you Libras who have been in a settled relationship for some time, this is a day when the question of marriage may arise. Making plans for the special day can be fun.

Saturday the 13th. General lethargy may be due to overwork or expending too much energy on other people. Take care of yourself for a change. Try not to postpone writing important letters any longer, for instance, renewing insurance policies. Looking after an elderly dependent can be exhausting, but it is up to you to ask for help when you need it.

Sunday the 14th. Even if you are busy, try to make a point of getting some fresh air and exercise. This does not have to be anything especially strenuous; a walk in the park can blow away the cobwebs. Later hours in the day can be favorable for entertaining at home. Aim for a casual occasion. Someone may want to confide a personal matter and be eager for your opinion.

Weekly Summary

Life is full of paradoxes, and if anyone can balance them out, you Libras can. You may have a full plate of exciting challenges this week. Those of you who work in creative fields probably know how difficult it can be to honor and nurture your creative process and make a living all at the same time. Make sure that the people you entrust with your work, whether they be agents, consultant advisers, managers, or salespeople, are giving you as much time and energy as they claim. If they are not, it may be worthwhile for you to do everything on your own. However much of a strain that may be, it can turn out that your own charm opens more doors than anybody else's.

This weekend can be your most productive time as far as practical matters are concerned. Try not to get compulsive about pushing too many errands or tasks into too tight a schedule. Getting things done around the house may be easier, especially on Saturday, than trying to accomplish tasks that involve a lot of running around. Those of you who have waited until the last minute to complete your tax returns may actually feel up to tackling the job on Sunday. If you have any questions, a family member may be able to help.

16th Week/April 15–21

Monday the 15th. Get pressing tasks out of the way early. Extra work can land on your desk just when you have managed to catch your breath. If certain individuals are not pulling their weight, this may be a good time for some tactful delegation. If you are at home, this can be a good opportunity to get to know new neighbors; they will appreciate some local information.

Tuesday the 16th. If you feel someone is trying to undermine your confidence, do not hesitate to stand up for yourself. You Libras who are studying for exams can benefit from some uninterrupted work. Let others know that you are not to be disturbed. Sharing a house has its ups and downs. This will be a good time for introducing a duty roster for the chores.

Wednesday the 17th. While some daydreaming is natural, you may need to make an extra effort not to let your work suffer. Employ some skepticism in your business dealings. Remind yourself that there is no such thing as a free lunch; someone's true motives may still be under wraps. Steer clear of alcohol this evening; you may confide in the wrong person.

Thursday the 18th. Unexpected expenses can put your finances under strain. Avoid taking out a loan unless you are sure that you can meet the payments. A child's bad behavior may be the result of problems at school. Your best policy is to encourage the youngster to confide in you. Thus you will be able to see how you can help; discipline is likely to have an adverse effect.

Friday the 19th. Person-to-person business meetings can be even more productive than you hoped for. Fears that you have lost a valued customer may be unfounded. This can be a favorable time for embarking on a course of study to improve your career prospects, but do not underestimate how time-consuming this can be. This evening lends itself to intimate get-togethers.

Saturday the 20th. This can be a favorable time for planning your next vacation. Keep an eye out for the places that offer activities for youngsters. A babysitting service can also make a lot of difference. You may decide on a trip to the theater or the movies this evening, but do not rely on last-minute availability. Book your tickets in advance over the telephone.

Sunday the 21st. This can be a good time for making long-distance telephone calls and catching up on all the news. Academic pursuits of all kinds can be stimulating. Mixing with people from different cultures can be educational. You Libras who have a new partner will find this a good day for meeting other members of the family; you should find that you hit it off together.

Weekly Summary

Partnership issues are always important to you Libras, but perhaps especially now. Those of you who are in the midst of confusing or strenuous times with the people who are closest to you may get some important insights into what is going wrong. These are tricky times. It may appear as though all the rules of the game are changing. Honest communication can be the key you are looking for. Your old Libra habit of backsliding or smoothing things over to avoid conflicts is unlikely to cause you anything but more problems right now, particularly with people who have authority over you. That Libra charm may have to give way to more direct ways of getting your point across. Pay close attention to all interpersonal dynamics on Wednesday. The New Moon may have a lesson to teach you about seeing things as they are now, rather than as they used to be.

A new cycle begins on Friday, and it can be helpful for those of you who want to keep your finances in order. Now that the tax season has theoretically passed, you may find it worthwhile to organize all your financial records so that they are easy to update on a weekly or monthly basis.

17th Week/April 22–28

Monday the 22nd. Do not drag your feet over certain matters; someone may be getting impatient. A colleague with whom you have never seen eye-to-eye can be a thorn in your side. Accept that you are probably never going to be best friends; but making a greater effort to understand the character of the person will be helpful. Money owing to you may be repaid.

Tuesday the 23rd. Clients who are normally elusive may be open to making specific appointments. This can be a propitious day for interviewing for an open position. Someone who is ambitious may be better than someone else with a stack of qualifications. If you have gone as far as you can go in your current job, this can be a favorable day for looking for a new position.

Wednesday the 24th. Prepare yourself for a disappointment at work. A feeling of frustration or injustice will probably go deep, but remind yourself that there is probably no point in resisting decisions over which you have no control. People in authority may have a tendency to be critical. This can be a symptom of their own pressures, so turn a deaf ear to their complaints.

Thursday the 25th. You probably need the support of your colleagues if you want any complaints taken seriously. If you are married, this is a time when you should avoid making social arrangements without consulting your spouse. He or she may be annoyed if committed to something the person would rather not do.

Friday the 26th. You Libras who belong to a political organization can find this a good time for canvassing; there is a chance of convincing others of the integrity of your policies. If you are seeking to extend your social circle, this can be a favorable time for joining a new club. Think twice about letting a special friendship develop into romance.

Saturday the 27th. Avoid lending money to friends, especially to a certain individual who has a reputation for being slow to repay debts. Lending out your personal possessions, such as clothes or music, can also be risky; there is a chance of something being broken or spoiled. A lost object may have to be written off. Missing someone who has recently moved can be painful.

Sunday the 28th. A brother or sister can be a tower of strength when it comes to confiding an emotional or ethical dilemma. The advice you receive will reveal an obvious answer and take a weight off your mind. Looking over old family photographs can evoke amusing memories. You Libras who are mechanically minded can find this a good time for working on your cars.

Weekly Summary

Business and professional concerns will take the lion's share of your attention in the early part of this week. Those of you who work closely with a partner or colleague probably do not need to be reminded of the pros and cons of your arrangement. While partners may help you to discipline your activities, guard against making more compromises than are really necessary. As your astrological chart reflects in so many different ways right now, honest communication is of the utmost importance. Those of you who are used to getting your way by obscuring the truth will probably not be able to pull that off much longer.

For you Libras who are involved in social action or humanitarian movements, this can be a week for caution. The image of your organization can easily suffer if you allow yourselves to be irresponsible or frivolous with money or media attention. Allow the highest ideals and beliefs of your group to guide you toward appropriate statements and activities. And remember to nip any form of prejudice or intolerance in the bud. Deal with divisiveness in your own group before you set yourselves up as models for others.

18th Week/April 29–May 5

Monday the 29th. Take steps to ensure that confidential information is not leaked to the wrong people. A certain individual may be deliberately keeping you in the dark. For you Libras who work in the performing arts, this can be a productive day. A new contract can be exciting; but wait until everything is signed before you start celebrating. Avoid telling white lies.

Tuesday the 30th. You cannot expect someone to ask you out unless you show that you are interested. Maybe the time has come for you to stick your neck out. Be encouraging and take a few calculated risks. Children can be delightful company; their innocent words can reflect poignantly on an issue in your own life and make you look at something in a new light.

Wednesday May 1st. Pushing too hard to get your own way can result in animosity. Resolve to meet someone halfway. This can be a favorable day for dealing with legal matters, especially those that involve recouping costs. For you Libras who work in the performing arts, this can be a lucky day for auditions; but the competition may be greater than anticipated.

Thursday the 2nd. While you cannot fight other people's battles for them, you may be able to defuse a heated argument. Guard against spending too much. This is unlikely to be a good time for making changes to your personal appearance. If you are having your hair cut, do not allow yourself to be talked into a new look unless you are sure that it is what you want.

Friday the 3rd. There is a risk of a secret being leaked. This may be a time when it would be better to bring everything out into the open anyway. Do not give someone the chance to think ill of you; give your side of the story first. An argument concerning joint finances may be brewing. If you know that you have been spending recklessly, there is no point to deny it.

Saturday the 4th. A new romance may be getting off to a slow start. Do not fall into the trap of sitting by the telephone and waiting for it to ring. It will do no harm for someone to know that you are not always instantly available. A new hobby or interest can be absorbing. You probably will benefit from studying with a group rather than on your own.

Sunday the 5th. This can be the perfect morning for going back to bed with the newspapers or a good book. You Libra students will find this a good day for taking a break from your studies; treat yourself to getting out or reading just for pleasure instead. Later hours in the day can be good for writing letters or making social arrangements over the telephone.

Weekly Summary

Big changes are in the offing this week. The first, which occurs on Thursday, is likely to trigger off activity in your financial life. Those of you whose investments and other long-term holdings are shared with family members or partners may be wise to prepare yourselves for some conflicts. If you do not see eye-to-eye, it may inadvisable to rush into any important decisions. Do not allow agents or sales executives to push you into commitments that do not feel right to all concerned. Remember, it is your money.

The next cycle is always important to be aware of, as it usually occurs about three times a year. From Friday until the 27th of the month, you can expect delays, misunderstanding, and general chaos with all of the details of daily life. This is no time to take anything for granted, especially not the mail, telephone, public transportation, or machinery of any kind. The fact that this shift coincides with the Full Moon can make it that much more frustrating. Negotiations and creative work can flourish during this time. However, practical decisions made now may have to be adjusted later on.

19th Week/May 6–12

Monday the 6th. If you are at home today, this can be a good time for doing some gardening. Houseplants probably will benefit from being repotted. Libra employees may find a superior more exacting than usual. Some tasks may take longer than you have allowed for. You may not feel like putting in overtime this evening; but the extra money can come in handy.

Tuesday the 7th. Rely on your hunches; instinctive decisions are likely to be the right ones. Money can come to you now. Remind yourself that it is an inescapable law that you get back what you give out. This can be an excellent time for investing money, whether it is a lump sum or monthly premiums.

Wednesday the 8th. If you have to fill in forms of any kind, make sure that you are scrupulously honest; a white lie can cause you some embarrassment. A frantic pace at work this afternoon is likely to keep you on your toes. If a colleague is snappy, it is probably due to working under pressure. Try to be tolerant of a loved one's nagging or pointless questions.

Thursday the 9th. Remember that gentle discipline is essential for a child's sense of boundaries as well as your sanity. Try to look for the cause of bad behavior rather than just punishing the symptoms. If your romance is on the rocks, guard against hanging on just for the sake of it. Be careful with money this evening.

Friday the 10th. A proposal to work abroad may be worth serious consideration. The new opportunity can be worth the upheaval; remind yourself that some sacrifice is usually necessary if you want to move on. A work problem may fall to you to sort out; this may mean having to stay on later than usual. Let a loved one know if you are going to be really late.

Saturday the 11th. This can be a good time for a relaxing day at home; do the usual chores at your own pace without putting yourself under unnecessary pressure. This can be a propitious day if you are looking for a place to live. Follow up a lead from someone at work; there is a good chance that it is just what you have had in mind. The evening favors entertaining at home.

Sunday the 12th. Browsing around the market can be fun even if you do not buy anything. If you are suffering from the ill effects of a heavy night out, make a point of taking some gentle physical exercise; this may be just what you need to chase away the sluggishness. Devote some time to a hobby or just relaxing.

Weekly Summary

This is likely to be a dynamic week. Allow yourself to take the time to release pent-up feelings that may be triggered off. This can be a healing time if you can open up to family members whom you may have been unconsciously avoiding for some time.

Nothing can be quite as disruptive as falling in love. However, this is especially true if you are already married or in a long-standing committed relationship. It can be a mistake to assume that an affair that starts now will stand the test of time. What is more likely is that it will make you see how much you are changing. Is your relationship keeping up? While it is always important to be true to yourself, if that means hurting someone else in the process, you had better think twice. Ask yourself, what do you really want? Make sure you are not barking up the wrong tree.

Things should settle down somewhat by the weekend. Those of you who have not been sure whether you have been coming or going will probably welcome anything resembling a normal routine. Saturday looks like a good time to tackle chores around the house. Sunday looks good for paying bills and getting up to date with your correspondence.

20th Week/May 13–19

Monday the 13th. This will be a propitious time for joining forces with a previous competitor. If you have recently split up with a partner, this is a day when you should feel that you are back on the road to recovery. A new romance can be on the horizon; it may be that someone is waiting for you to notice. You married Libras should enjoy an evening with your spouse.

Tuesday the 14th. This can be a good day for working closely with your staff. Your support can be the key to sorting out problems. You are more likely to find out what someone really thinks in one-to-one meetings. You Libras who are unattached may be asked out. Even if there is not an immediate attraction, you may find this relationship will grow slowly but firmly.

Wednesday the 15th. Financial gambles of any kind should be avoided; stay with the tried and trusted or take expert advice. This can be a difficult time for pushing for a raise; take promises with a pinch of salt. Avoid laying down ultimatums unless you already have another job lined up. This is not a good time for walking out in high dudgeon. Arrangements for child care need to be confirmed.

Thursday the 16th. This can be a good time for assessing the security of your own home; ask yourself if it is as burglar-proof as you think. It may be worth investing in some strong locks for doors or windows. This evening can be a good time for going for a drink straight from work with colleagues or your friends.

Friday the 17th. If your marriage is going through an unacceptably long bad patch, this can be the time to take decisive action. The idea of a counselor may be alien to you; but an objective professional can sort out problems that have had you stumped. Bringing difficulties out into the open can be a relief This evening can be favorable for the movies or a night spot.

Saturday the 18th. You may have forgotten how much you enjoy the company of a certain individual. Have your camera on hand for any social event; photographs taken now are likely to come out particularly well. In this way you can keep happy memories fresh. This can be the perfect day for starting a vacation. If you have a partner, treat him or her to a romantic dinner this evening.

Sunday the 19th. You Libras who are at the point of announcing your wedding plans will find this a favorable day for meeting your prospective in-laws. Family input for your special day can be important, but make sure that the final arrangements are what you and your partner really want. If you are taking children on an outing, aim for something educational.

Weekly Summary

As the spotlight falls on your close partnerships this week, you may want to take some inventory on how you are doing. You Libras are in the midst of a cycle where you can find yourselves wavering between dependence and independence. While getting along with other people is vital to your well-being, some people are simply not easy to relate to. If someone in your life insists on doing everything the hard way, that doesn't necessarily mean you have to follow suit. Monday look for creative solutions you can both live with.

As the summer vacation season is fast approaching, this is probably a reasonable time to think about what you want to do this year. Try not to let obligations to other people hold you back from taking some well-deserved time off. Even the most demanding employers know how vital it is to take advantage of holidays. If you are planning to go abroad, make sure you check out the political climate as well as the meteorological climate before you book your tickets. The last thing you need is to get embroiled in a sticky situation which hampers your freedom of movement.

21st Week/May 20–26

Monday the 20th. If meetings or other appointments are canceled, you should be able to put your unexpected free time to good use. A job offer can come your way. It may not sound very exciting; but once you have a foot in the door, it can lead to more interesting work. An older relative can be prove to be a fountain of wisdom in connection with a personal issue.

Tuesday the 21st. You Libra women who want to return to work after having a baby may want to look into the prospect of job sharing. If your career is not progressing in the way you were hoping, now can be a favorable time for talking with a superior; there is no point in keeping your grievances to yourself. Friction at home can be resolved if you talk honestly.

Wednesday the 22nd. This should be an excellent time for considering volunteer work. In this way you can put yourself in contact with new people. Your efforts can also be helpful when it comes to impressing a future employer. Business dealings with overseas contacts can be frustrating at present. It may be time to arrange a trip so you can confer with people directly.

Thursday the 23rd. Certain individuals may be deliberately stirring up bad feeling to serve their own ends. It is probably up to you to bring their true motives to light. Discussions can quickly turn into heated arguments. Money can be a sensitive issue. If you are out with friends this evening, make sure that you do not pick up more than your fair share of the bill.

Friday the 24th. A fund-raising event can attract greater crowds and publicity than anticipated. A celebrity from the world of film or theater may be willing to lend both name and support to an advertising campaign. Try not to be intimidated by someone's fame when it comes to making the first approach. Old school friends can get in touch today about a reunion.

Saturday the 25th. This is likely to be a sociable day. Even if you have not made any definite plans to see anyone, friends may just turn up on the doorstep. A spontaneous outing can be great fun. There is a chance of an old romance being rekindled. While it is natural to have some reservations, you can be lucky the second time around if you clear up misunderstandings.

Sunday the 26th. A strange dream may be trying to tell you something; taking heed of your unconscious can be revealing. This can be a favorable day for turning your hand to some home decorating. A fresh coat of paint can do a lot to brighten up a room. Cleaning out old cupboards can also be helpful. But do not be too ruthless; keep some items for old times' sake.

Weekly Summary

Two planetary shifts dominate this week's astrological events. The first, which occurs on Monday, is likely to be felt as a kind of excitement or anticipation. We all need something to look forward to, and these little glimmerings from inside may remind you to seek out greater happiness. You can call it spring fever. Whatever it is, you are entering a cycle where the operating question is where are you going in life. Reconnect with the goals that make you excited about life. Perhaps you have always wanted to travel to a certain far-off land, study a religion that holds a special fascination, or study a subject that you find especially interesting. Even if you can take only the smallest step toward realizing your dream, that may be enough for now.

The next cycle, which starts on Tuesday and lasts until early July, may signal the beginning of a potentially introverted phase. You hardworking Libra professionals who are also burdened by family concerns are cautioned to make sure you have enough time on your own. This weekend looks ideal for solitude. Daydream, meditate, be an armchair traveler.

22nd Week/May 27–June 2

Monday the 27th. Walking at least part of the way to work can give you some peaceful time for your own thoughts before other matters take over. This can be a favorable day for working by telephone. A cheerful manner should get you past the toughest of secretaries. A superior may frown on too much jollity in the office. Just make sure that the real work gets done to the required standard.

Tuesday the 28th. Take extra trouble with your personal appearance. Abandon a new outfit in favor of something more conventional. A recent success at work will make you feel justifiably proud of yourself. Unfortunately, you may not get the praise from others that you deserve. Try not to be crushed; the important thing is to know you have done an exemplary job.

Wednesday the 29th. A degree course may appeal to you Libras who have been out of mainline education for some time. But it will be wise to discuss this with your partner before you make any definite decisions. Be realistic about the demands that the studying may make on your time or the strains that it may put on your relationship. Try to recognize your real priorities.

Thursday the 30th. Money matters loom large now. If this is payday, you may find that there is a little extra in your pay envelope. This may be due to overtime pay or a tax refund. This can be a favorable time for working out your budget for the coming month. Saving for your summer vacation or for something special can be a great incentive to spend more carefully.

Friday the 31st. Double-check all financial moves being made on your behalf. Do not take the risk of driving without full insurance; there is a chance of being caught. This can be a good time for a safety check on your car; for instance, make sure that all your tires are up to standard. A promised telephone call for this evening may not happen.

Saturday June 1st. Shopping in the neighborhood can leave you more time to hang out at home. Later on, call or write to friends or family who live abroad. Family matters may be high on the agenda. A long chat with a brother or sister can make you aware of a problem you knew nothing about. Your arbitration skills may come in handy. This evening can be good for dressing up and going out.

Sunday the 2nd. You Libra full-time students are advised to devise a study program and stick to it. This might mean having to forgo some social events; but remind yourself that this is only in the short term. Be tactful about airing your political or religious beliefs. A simple opinion can be taken for an inflammatory remark. A visitor from overseas is sure to appreciate your hospitality.

Weekly Summary

Those of you who have been exasperated by delays, disruptions, and misunderstandings for the past few weeks can breathe a sigh of relief. That irritating cycle that has caused communication breakdowns and general pandemonium around the details of daily life comes to an end on Monday.

Otherwise, the focus this week is on you. Whatever personal projects you have been wanting to get off the ground, talents or skills you want to develop, this is probably a good time to get started. Look to the future, not to the past, for the answers you seek. Insecurities from childhood can only hold you back. Unfortunately, this may also be true of well-meaning family members who are reluctant to let you go. You are in a cycle where your conviction and fortitude are likely to be tested. Try to concern yourself more with what you think than what other people think.

As far as money is concerned, those of you who get a weekly paycheck are advised to make sure it does not burn a hole in your pocket. The tendency to over-spend will be strong on Thursday and Friday.

23rd Week/June 3–9

Monday the 3rd. Interruptions can make it difficult to concentrate. It may be wise to leave more demanding tasks for tomorrow. Be realistic about committing yourself to deadlines; you may realize too late that you have put yourself under too much pressure. The same applies to your social life. Invitations can be tempting; but there is a risk of overstretching yourself.

Tuesday the 4th. Guard against leaping to conclusions when it comes to analyzing other people's behavior; there is a chance that you are wrong. Remind yourself that clear communication is the essential ingredient in every relationship, whether it is a personal or a pro-fessional one. If you want to know something, the best way is simply to ask a direct question.

Wednesday the 5th. This should be an excellent time for winding up a legal matter that has been going on for a long time. Even if you cannot bring something to a conclusion, you should be able to make significant strides in the right direction. If you have not yet booked a summer vacation, this can be a favorable time for scouting around for last-minute offers.

Thursday the 6th. Be careful that you do not confide in the wrong people about your personal problems. Partners may not take kindly to the fact that they have been discussed; words can be fed back to them in the wrong context. For you Libra parents, this is a time to be aware of telltale signs of bullying. If you are wor-ried that your child is a victim, intervene now.

Friday the 7th. This is likely to be a low-key end to the working week. This can be a good time for making routine health appointments, for instance, dental treatment or a sight test. If you have always worn glasses, you may consider making the switch to contact lenses. If you are not in the mood for cooking this evening, have a meal out or get something nice to take away.

Saturday the 8th. Domestic chores may be piling up; but you may not have the energy or the inclination to tackle them. Try to discipline yourself to do the most pressing ones. The initial powerful attraction of a new romance can be wearing off. It may be that you are discovering that you do not have that much in common. It will help to take up an outside interest.

Sunday the 9th. You Libras usually prefer company. But try not to rely too heavily on someone else for your entertainment. You can find that you enjoy an outing more by yourself; this way you do not have to worry about someone else getting bored or irritable. A friend or family member may be willing to take the kids off your hands for the afternoon.

Weekly Summary

You Libra people who have children in your care can probably look forward to an enjoyable time together this week. Take advantage of all the resources in the community that can inspire and expand your mutual horizons. Even young children can often get something out of a visit to a live theater, museum, dance performance, or art gallery. You may discover you have a budding young talent on your hands. Wednesday afternoon looks ideal for going exploring together.

Later on, those of you who are stuck in the same old job or household routine are likely to find yourselves yearning for something more. Try to be philosophical about your predicament; resolve to get involved in a study or activity that is meaningful to you. If financial restraints prevent you from having as much freedom as you would like, set aside some time on the weekend to get your accounts in order. Once you know where you are, you can devise a step-by-step program to get yourself out of your rut. Saving for the future can be a joy when working toward a goal that inspires you.

24th Week/June 10–16

Monday the 10th. Business meetings can be productive if you allow enough time to reach agreements. If you are entertaining a client to lunch, steer clear of expensive places. Although the occasion can be great fun, the size of the bill may be alarming. This evening lends itself to a restful time at home watching television.

Tuesday the 11th. Sudden changes of routine can be foisted upon you, but these can turn out to be enjoyable. If you work in the world of film or television, the chance to meet a celebrity will be exciting. This afternoon can be good for browsing around a market. Make a point of visiting the book stalls; you may find something valuable at a fraction of the usual price.

Wednesday the 12th. This can be a good time to take expert financial advice. For you Libra first-time buyers, this can be a propitious day for sorting out a mortgage; you should find that the transaction goes through smoothly and quickly. Some help with the deposit can be forthcoming from a relative. If you are looking for a new job, do not undervalue the perks.

Thursday the 13th. An ambitious business proposal may be more viable than it first appears; be prepared to investigate it thoroughly lest you miss out on a magical opportunity. For you Libra employees who work on a flexible schedule, this can be the perfect time to take the morning off. The afternoon may be strenuous. Letters or contracts may have to be rewritten.

Friday the 14th. This can be a tiring day. Hours of work can strain your powers of concentration. Business negotiations can be tough if you are dealing with a customer over the telephone. Guard against pushing too hard; there is a risk of coming away with nothing to show for all your efforts. Patience is more likely to win results. Pass on important telephone messages.

Saturday the 15th. Do not fall into the trap of believing that your working life will come to a screaming halt without you; nobody is that indispensable, and everybody needs a break from routine. Avoid relying on someone else to get tickets for a night out; you can be disappointed. A party this evening can be good fun, but avoid getting trapped by people who want you to solve their problems.

Sunday the 16th. A change of scenery can be refreshing. Make a point of fitting in what you normally consider to be a duty call, perhaps to a neighbor or to in-laws. This can turn out to be surprisingly good fun. The company of those who are well informed and love to debate can challenge your own beliefs. Be prepared to enter into intellectual discussions.

Weekly Summary

Those of you who are involved in taking financial risks, whether it be on the stock market or at the racetrack, are advised to exercise some self-control this week. If someone offers you a gift horse, this is one time you may want to reject the offer. Your ability to see through other people's false masks is strong right now. Make use of it. First make sure their intentions are honorable. If appropriate, proceed with caution, following your gut feelings every step of the way.

A new cycle begins on Wednesday and is likely to trigger off activity on the international front. That will make this a good week for you Libras who want to expand your professional horizons. If competition is especially fierce right now, why not explore untapped opportunities in foreign markets? If you do not already speak a foreign language, this will be the ideal time to get started. Even if future clients speak your language, you have a greater chance of understanding one another on a deeper level if you can communicate in their native tongue.

25th Week/June 17–23

Monday the 17th. Be prepared to be thrown in at the deep end at work. For you Libra parents who work full time, this can be a favorable day for making child care arrangements for the summer. Find out about play groups in your local neighborhood; the library may have some useful information. If you are a single parent, you may qualify for subsidized activities for your child.

Tuesday the 18th. If a personal matter is on your, mind you may find it difficult to concentrate. This sort of experience can remind you of what your true priorities are. Once you regain a sense of perspective, you will feel more cheerful and able to cope. This afternoon can be good for meetings with colleagues; teamwork of all kinds can be both productive and enjoyable.

Wednesday the 19th. If you are planning to travel this summer, this can be a good day to make sure that your passport and visas are in order. Embassies of the countries you intend to visit can provide you with useful information. Learning a second language can be fun. Any endeavors at self-improvement can have the added bonus of extending your social circle.

Thursday the 20th. Make a point of keeping in touch with those people whose company you always enjoy. If your working life has been boring lately, you may consider setting yourself some new goals. If you are ready for a career change, some professional guidance will be helpful. Be prepared to take a drop in salary if you have to retrain for a job you would love to do.

Friday the 21st. You may not see eye-to-eye with a certain individual at first, but you should be able to reach an acceptable compromise if you are prepared to hear each other out. Guard against interrupting. If you have a medical appointment, do not hesitate to ask any questions you need. This evening can be good for trying out foreign cuisine you have never tasted before.

Saturday the 22nd. There is a danger that you will feel under the weather this morning. You professional Libras may be suffering from the results of overwork; make a point of switching off completely this weekend. Even if you did bring work home with you, it can probably wait. Your own company can be the most enjoyable this evening.

Sunday the 23rd. Looking over old photographs from your childhood can bring back some amusing memories. You Libras who have recently split from a partner may now be regretting your decision; maybe you acted in the heat of the moment. An attempt at reconciliation probably will not be turned down; do not let pride stand in your way.

Weekly Summary

This looks like a good week for expanding your circle of friends. People who share your ideals and vision of the future can be a real boost right now. Those of you who have not been having an easy time with your close partners can probably benefit from spending some time with people who accept you as you are. You Libras are in the midst of an important transformation in your willingness and ability to communicate. Follow your inner cues. The more frank you are in telling your stories, the more other people will be able to understand and help you. Get together any time between Tuesday afternoon through Thursday.

Friday marks the beginning of a cycle that is bound to shed some light on your career. Those of you who have professional meetings scheduled may do well to observe more than participate. This is one time when knowing when to keep your mouth shut can make all the difference. Use your intuition before you blurt out any information that may have been best kept confidential. If you are about to launch an advertising or public relations campaign, you must be absolutely sure that everyone involved can be trusted.

26th Week/June 24–30

Monday the 24th. Your efforts to play fair may be holding you back at work; a certain individual may not hesitate to take advantage of your understanding nature. Realize that there are occasions where you have to push your own needs and interests to the forefront. A legal matter may be dragging on; a favorable outcome is likely if you are patient.

Tuesday the 25th. Make sure that someone who is attracted to you is sincere before you commit yourself to going out together. Charm can be superficial. Try to be realistic about your eating habits. There is a danger of giving in to temptation. If you are hunting an apartment, take agents' descriptions with a pinch of salt; learn to read between the lines.

Wednesday the 26th. If you have never tried to save in the past, this can be a good time to start. Even a small amount each month can soon mount up; this way you will never be without a safety net. If you are married, this is a day when your spouse may be anxious about his or her job; maybe there is a threat of redundancy. Think of ways in which you can provide against this eventuality.

Thursday the 27th. This can be a good time for shopping for household goods. But resist the temptation to take on credit unless it is free of interest. If you are unemployed, you may consider working for yourself as an alternative to looking for another job. Someone who has already made this move can provide useful advice about your tax and insurance situation.

Friday the 28th. Anticipate train cancellations or severe traffic jams. Take extra care with finished written or creative work; spilling a cup of coffee can spell disaster. Think twice about returning persistent telephone calls from someone you would rather not see; they may get the message and get off your back. An impromptu arrangement can lead to a great night out.

Saturday the 29th. This can be a frustrating day. If your car is on its last legs, you may have to face the fact that it is not worth fixing. The telephone can be busy, but you may not hear from the one person you are waiting for. Try not to let the disappointment spoil the rest of the day. An evening out with an old friend may not work out; perhaps your interests have developed along different lines.

Sunday the 30th. If home decorating is long overdue, you can make a start now. Rope in your partner or a friend to speed things up. If you are entertaining, you may be feeling the strain of playing host. Someone may be oblivious to the amount of work you are putting in. It cannot do any harm to ask pointedly for some help. An argument with a loved one may seem insoluble; sleep on it.

Weekly Summary

You may be feeling the benefit of recent bouts of independence. But it may be helpful to be sensitive to the fact that certain people would prefer to maintain control over your comings and goings. There is a price to pay for freedom. Sometimes security is only the down payment.

You Libras often have a soft spot for beautiful things. If you can afford them, why not? However, there can be a tendency to go overboard this week as far as your personal spending is concerned. Wednesday can be critical in this regard. Those of you who are responsible for purchasing computers or other hi-tech professional equipment are advised to take things slow and easy. Stay away from short-term special offers. Somebody may try to dump questionable equipment.

Those of you who are working on written or oral presentations should be able to make some real headway later in the week. Concentration and perseverance are two keys to success in this area. Follow your hunches, and allow yourself room to put your personal stamp on the final product. Your prospective client is sure to appreciate total honesty. Do not hesitate to share your insights or opinions even though they may be controversial.

27th Week/July 1–7

Monday July 1st. This can be a good day for doing some gardening or just for lying around in the sun. Concentrate on tying up the loose ends of projects that are coming to a close. You probably will not be in the mood for going too far afield this evening. Relaxing to your favorite music or watching television may be appealing, especially if you have had a busy weekend.

Tuesday the 2nd. Get to know someone well before you pass on confidential information. It may be wiser to hang back when it comes to putting a business proposition to someone until you have thought through the possible consequences. Your partner can be in an unpredictable mood. Make an effort to listen carefully if he or she wants to talk about something.

Wednesday the 3rd. Taking a day off from work is unlikely to go down well with a superior. If a letter you are expecting does not turn up, see if it was mailed in the first place. A job interview can go well if you guard against complacency. Someone seems determined to put you through your paces. Do not exaggerate your achievements; stick to the unvarnished truth.

Thursday the 4th. Earning money now can mean that you will be able to travel or take a proper vacation later on in the summer. For you Libras who are unattached, this can be a lucky time for meeting someone new. Or there may be a romance blossoming with someone you have known for a long time, maybe from childhood. Children can be fun this holiday.

Friday the 5th. Guard against making lame excuses or passing the buck; someone can be more kindly disposed toward you if you accept responsibility for errors. A work function may be unappealing, but you cannot afford to let a superior notice your absence. At least put in a token appearance, if only to show interest. Try to avoid taking work home with you.

Saturday the 6th. Make yourself available if someone is struggling with a genuine crisis even if it is inconvenient. Libra parents will find this afternoon good for a children's party or an outing. Little ones are likely to be on their best behavior. It may be up to you to cheer up your partner this evening; make a point of suggesting something specific that you can enjoy together.

Sunday the 7th. A family get-together can have tense moments; there may be issues going on under the surface of which you are not fully informed. Avoid getting caught in the middle or being tempted to take sides. Let others sort out their own differences. For you married Libras, a trip to see in-laws can be fun in the right frame of mind. Enjoy being wined and dined.

Weekly Summary

While there may be other problems or challenges on your mind, you Libras should be feeling pretty good this week. Your ruling planet Venus, which has been operating at somewhat of a disadvantage since the third week in May, gets back on course on Tuesday. Those of you who have been feeling unsure about your relationships or a bit awkward with other people can look forward to easier times ahead.

Working in offices can be frustrating for anybody at times. However, when you are forced to work with someone you do not trust, it can be unbearable. If this description fits your situation in any way, shape, or form, this may be the time to start doing something about it. Any complaints you make to people in charge are likely to be taken more seriously if you can come up with and recommend a practical solution. This is probably no time to get too emotional. To do so can severely damage your professional credibility. Tread carefully, and make use of your famous Libra tact and diplomacy. However, do not withhold uncomfortable facts that will force a decision in your favor.

28th Week/July 8–14

Monday the 8th. If someone is behaving irrationally, there is probably little that you can say that will make any difference. Sometimes you just have to watch others make their own mistakes. You single Libras who have been nursing a secret passion for someone may find that your feelings are on the wane. A child may not be able to articulate a problem; let the youngster know you understand.

Tuesday the 9th. If you are offered a temporary job, it may be worth taking, even if you have been thinking of something more permanent. This can be an excellent day for public speaking, for instance, delivering a lecture or presentation. This is likely to be a good time for placing advertisements; go for top-quality publications with a proven track record.

Wednesday the 10th. Refuse to rise to the bait if someone tries to antagonize you in any way. This is not a day for rushing at things. Most problems can have easy solutions if you are prepared to stop and think before you act. If you are in the process of house hunting, this is a good day for finalizing financial details. Shop around for a preferential rate of interest.

Thursday the 11th. Secondhand bookshops are worth a visit; you Libra students can come across some useful texts for a fraction of the price. If you have suddenly decided that you want to return to full-time education, this can be a good time for exploring the possibilities. Find out if you are eligible for a grant or scholarship. A holiday romance may continue once the vacation is over.

Friday the 12th. Try not to enter into arguments about politics; they can get far too heated for comfort. Bad feelings on both sides can linger on for far too long. At work, guard against being overcompetitive. In fact, it can pay dividends to let someone else take the limelight unchallenged. You Libra actors may find that an audition is more grueling than anticipated.

Saturday the 13th. If you have not made any definite plans, you may consider taking yourself off to an art exhibit or museum. This can be enjoyable whether you go alone or with someone who shares your tastes. If you are planning to take a vacation, this can be a favorable time for finding a package deal with a healthy discount. An invitation to dine out will come as an unexpected treat.

Sunday the 14th. If you feel your partner is not being honest with you, it may help to point out that you cannot resolve any difficulties if either of you is trying to cover up mistakes. Be prepared to examine your own behavior, no matter how uncomfortable this can make you feel. Someone in the family may be unwilling to reveal a work problem. Try to be sensitive.

Weekly Summary

As far as money is concerned, this can be a lucky week for those of you who are involved in real estate. Waterfront property will be especially worthy of your time and attention. Tuesday and Wednesday can bring important opportunities in this regard. Keep your eyes and ears open. It may take some imagination to see the potential in properties that have been abandoned.

Long-distance love affairs are not out of the question this summer. You Libras are likely to meet attractive people in the most unexpected places these days. Love can strike any time and any place. However, try not to get deeply involved when you know there is no chance of anything lasting between you.

It may be hard to settle down and enjoy any semblance of domestic peace this weekend if professional concerns are weighing heavily on your mind. Those of you who have been neglecting your family will do well to focus your attention fully on them for once. Get your priorities straight. It is sometimes easy to forget why it is you are working so hard or for whom.

29th Week/July 15–21

Monday the 15th. If you are passed over for a promotion, try to be gracious and wait for the next opportunity. If you feel that you have gone as far as you can go in your current job, now can be a good time for casting around for a new position. This may be a good time for investing in some renovations at home. Avoid entrusting tasks to others; they are likely to forget.

Tuesday the 16th. Be prepared to defend your position and back up what you say with solid facts. This can be a good time for updating your office technology, for instance, more advanced computer software. Try to discourage friends from calling you at the office too frequently; someone in authority can take exception to your arranging your social life on work time.

Wednesday the 17th. Try to avoid overstretching yourself this week; there is a risk that you are trying to fit in too much. Make a point of clearing your vacation dates with colleagues so that you can be sure not to clash. For you Libra parents, you may have to cope with the ups and downs of adolescent behavior.

Thursday the 18th. You cannot take back harsh words, but a sincere apology will mean that they are quickly forgotten. Use a reliable delivery service for important mail; there is a danger of something going astray. This can be a confusing time when it comes to making career decisions. If you are not sure what you want to do, it may help to seek some professional guidance.

Friday the 19th. If you need to raise a delicate issue with someone, it will be wise to rehearse exactly what you want to say. Then there will be less risk of being sidetracked or misunderstood. An administrative error that has gone unnoticed may be the cause of the delay. A reunion with old school friends should be successful, but you have grown apart from one individual.

Saturday the 20th. This can be a good time for restoring old photographs or keepsakes from your childhood. A romantic relationship from the past can be revived. Enjoy seeing the person without worrying about old problems too much; it may be too early to judge how things will progress. Entertaining friends at home can be a better option than going out.

Sunday the 21st. Do not be possessive. Let your partner pursue his or her own interests while you pursue yours. A visit to your family may be more enjoyable if you go alone. This can be a favorable time for revamping your wardrobe. An old sweater or a pair of shoes can be dyed to a favorite color. Avoid tying yourself to the kitchen stove; eating out can be a welcome change.

Weekly Summary

Every new opportunity has its downside. Those of you who are lucky enough to be advancing in your careers are probably already aware of the sacrifices you have to make along the way. Monday's New Moon may find you feeling confused about your future direction. In all things, strive for balance. This is bound to be tricky.

An important planetary shift occurs on Thursday which is bound to be felt throughout the week. This will be a good time to remember that every cloud, no matter how dark, has a silver lining. Challenges and difficulties are always beneficial in that they help to clarify what may have been fuzzy situations. You Libras who are having problems in your personal and professional partnerships are advised to resolve to put increased effort into finding more solid common ground. When you are through with all this, you are all likely to be a bit older and wiser. By all means, do not allow yourself to let feelings of fear or insecurity take over. At least part of your future success will probably be based on your ability to recognize what you want and believe in and be ready to stand your own ground.

30th Week/July 22–28

Monday the 22nd. This can be an excellent day for a haircut; a new style can prove to be a great success even if it does take some getting used to. Work problems are best tackled with the assistance of others. You can pick up some useful ideas from a colleague who has more experience. This can be a good time for becoming a member of a charitable organization.

Tuesday the 23rd. You may find that you have more energy than usual and can get through a significant amount of work. If you are dieting, try not to succumb to temptation this afternoon. If you work with children, vary the activities even more than usual; staying too long on one subject can be a recipe for boredom and bad behavior. A social later may be postponed.

Wednesday the 24th. If someone is distracting you from your work, you may have to be direct if the message is going to get through. If you are applying for a loan, take extra care when filling in forms. An error on your part can delay the procedure. If you live in shared accommodations, this can be a good time for setting up a fund for communal expenses.

Thursday the 25th. This morning is likely to be the most productive time. Your plans for the afternoon can be subject to upheaval. A long-standing appointment may be canceled at short notice. Allow extra time for travel, even for short journeys; there is a risk of delays. Guard against parking illegally. If you are looking for a job, be prepared to take on something temporary.

Friday the 26th. If you owe a letter to an old friend, do not put it off any longer. This can be a productive day for you Libra salespeople who work over the telephone. Cold calling can produce unusually good results if you catch the right person at the right time. This can be a favorable time for finishing off written work, such as a report. A quiet evening is ahead.

Saturday the 27th. Refuse to be a passenger with someone whose driving you do not trust or if you suspect that the driver has had one too many drinks. You may be accident-prone in other ways; take extra care when crossing the road or navigating difficult stairs. Handle sharp instruments with respect. This evening can be a favorable time for a night out with a group.

Sunday the 28th. This can be a good day for gathering your family and loved ones around you. You may consider laying out a truly traditional Sunday; cook lunch with all the trimmings. Sitting around the table after eating can lead to interesting conversation. If you are a guest in someone else's home, make a point of pitching in when it comes to routine jobs.

Weekly Summary

Two important planetary shifts influence this week's astrological climate. The first, which occurs on Monday, summons the beginning of a month-long cycle which is bound to throw some light on your friendships and group involvements. Those of you who have strong humanitarian beliefs should feel free to express them fully. Letters you write to politicians and others involved in public policy may receive more attention than you ever hoped for. It is the squeaky wheel that gets oiled. Dramatic expressions of uncomfortable truths can help to open people's eyes.

Thursday marks the onset of another cycle. This one is likely to turn up the heat professionally. You Libras are not always the most ambitious people in the world. However, there are times when you may be forced to commit yourself to the maximum. Information may come to light this week which can have the effect of intensifying the competition. This might present conflicts for those of you who were hoping to get away about now. While there may be no reason to forgo your travel plans, it may be wise to stay in contact.

31st Week/July 29–August 4

Monday the 29th. There is unlikely to be anything of great urgency to deal with in the office now; you may be able to take a longer lunch break than usual. This afternoon should be a productive time for you Libra business people; departmental meetings can be wrapped up quickly and can produce some original ideas. If you have no plans this evening, how about meeting a small group of friends?

Tuesday the 30th. If you belong to a union, this can be a good time for taking any grievances to your official representative. Guard against trying to take the law into your own hands. Being at home with small children can be especially demanding. This can be a favorable time for finding out about play groups or babysitting circles to ease the strain.

Wednesday the 31st. Working with children can be fun, but you may find yourself fighting a losing battle when it comes to trying to control the noise level. If you are missing a loved one who is away, treat yourself to a long-distance phone call. The pressure at work is likely to be stepped up later in the day. Covering for a colleague who is sick can mean an increased work load.

Thursday August 1st. Working from home may be feasible, but find out about prices for renting commercial property. This can be a good time for relocating your business to a place where you can get more space for your money. In your personal life, this can be a day when you clash strongly with a loved one. Try not to lash out verbally; you may regret harsh words later on.

Friday the 2nd. An alternative remedy may not be working as quickly as you were hoping, but remind yourself to give it a fair trial. Steer clear of alcohol if you are taking medication of any kind; there is a risk of an adverse reaction. This can be a favorable time for raising a confidential issue with your employer. If you have started a new job, make sure that you get a written contract of terms and conditions.

Saturday the 3rd. Guard against playing the martyr role. Remind yourself that if you ask for nothing, that is exactly what you will get: nothing. This is likely to be a sociable day on the whole; friends may drop in on the chance of finding you at home. If you are throwing a party, keep a sharp eye out for gate-crashers.

Sunday the 4th. Before you go away on your summer vacation make sure that you leave your home secure. Timing devices for lights can be worth investing in. If there is no one whom you can trust with a key, then put your plants in a shallow bath; they should survive quite happily. Family talk about the past can be boring to your partner. If you are single, a new relationship can be brewing.

Weekly Summary

Those of you who have children in your care are almost sure to have a busy week. Staying up to date with a child's progress is always important. However, it can make all the difference if there are learning difficulties or just plain old-fashioned fears and insecurities. Creative, innovative teaching methods may be worth investigating. Remember that while some children thrive in traditional educational settings, others thrive on freedom. Try not to fall into the trap of comparing any two children. Keep in mind also that unusual talents are sometimes obscured by an inability to do simple tasks easily. The inevitable tensions associated with Tuesday's Full Moon may be worthwhile if it helps you see things in broader perspective.

You dedicated Libras who work in offices or in any of the helping professions can find yourselves doing some overtime this week. Vacation relief staff can come in really handy when unexpected difficulties arise behind the scenes. If your boss or supervisor is unwilling to cooperate, you may want to see what arrangements you can make among yourselves. Being forthright in your demands is bound to get the most satisfying results.

32nd Week/August 5–11

Monday the 5th. Some delicate juggling may be needed to meet your bills on time. You may be able to get an extension on certain bills to take off the immediate pressure. If you are self-employed, this can be a good time for a meeting with your accountant to come up with some suggestions to improve your cash flow. Avoid social arrangements that will cost you a lot.

Tuesday the 6th. This can be a favorable time for recognizing any obsessive or destructive behavior patterns. If you think you are drinking too much or overeating, now can be a good time to prove to yourself that you can stop. At work this can be a favorable time for improving your time management. Your boss may be willing to pay for you to attend courses.

Wednesday the 7th. Aim for an earlier train or bus to work; in this way you can avoid getting held up in traffic. Discourage neighbors from outstaying their welcome. You Libra managers are advised to avoid pulling rank. An attitude of superiority is sure to create bad feeling; you may get your own way at the cost of your popularity. Problems need to be met with patience and discretion.

Thursday the 8th. Legal decisions are likely to go in your favor. If you are unsure of your rights in any situation, this is a good time for getting advice. You Libra business people can find this a good time for arranging appointments in other cities or even other countries. A fund-raising drive for a charitable concern can get a start; good publicity is essential.

Friday the 9th. This is likely to be an easy day at work. News of a pending raise may be announced. If you are a sales representative, make sure that you put your expenses claim in. Later hours in the day can be good for shopping for new clothes; there is a good chance of finding what you want with very little effort. The theater or the movies can be enjoyable this evening.

Saturday the 10th. Dealing with the public can tax your powers of diplomacy; make an extra effort to remind yourself that the customer is always right. If you are out shopping, it may be best to avoid the main street; bigger crowds than usual can be frustrating and slow you down. If you are entertaining at home this evening, try to prepare most things well in advance.

Sunday the 11th. Make sure that those you live with pull their weight. You may consider paying someone to help out a few hours a week. If you work full-time, this can be an essential rather than a luxury. Someone close to you may be making light of a problem. You may suspect that you have not been given the full story, but there is no point in forcing the issue.

Weekly Summary

While you may think that the price you are paying is quite dear, there is probably no doubt that you Libras are growing up this year. Those of you who have had exceptionally romantic notions about relationships can be suffering from a loss of innocence in this regard. However, the relationships you form as a result of what you are learning now will almost certainly serve you well in the future. You are entering a cycle this week, which may make you particularly attractive to people who have authority over you.

Those of you who are planning a late summer romp in the countryside are advised to take extra care while driving. A powerful astrological aspect occurs on Saturday, and it is strong enough to influence the activities of the entire week. You Libras may already be going through changes that make it impossible for you to take any kind of travel for granted. However, this week can be critical. Be careful. Those of you who are in the midst of your summer vacation will be wise to reconfirm all your flight bookings. If you are traveling in a foreign country, make sure your embassy knows where you are.

33rd Week/August 12–18

Monday the 12th. Administrative matters can take up the best part of the morning. Make a point of being thoroughly prepared for meetings. Having certain facts at your fingertips will be the key to countering any opposition. This can be a good time for a mailing if you are launching a new product or advertising a special offer. An evening with an old friend can be fun.

Tuesday the 13th. If your social life is threatening to become nonexistent, take steps to improve it. Do not expect things to drop into your lap. Try to make some definite plans for the weekend. You can suggest doing something different like ice skating or having a picnic. If you are recently separated, do not lose touch with your friends. But you will soon be reaccepted.

Wednesday the 14th. Someone you have been working closely with can be developing into a firm friend and ally. This can be a good time for setting yourself achievable goals when it comes to furthering your career interests. Be prepared to drop your own plans if you can be of any help to someone close. The end of a relationship may be hard to accept.

Thursday the 15th. Shut your office door, and let it be known that you are not to be disturbed. You will be amazed at how much you can get through without interruptions. If you go out on a job interview, this can be a propitious day; you are almost certain to end up on the short list. You Libra employers may consider laying on more facilities for staff.

Friday the 16th. Make sure that you keep confidential information to yourself until it becomes official. For you Libras who are unattached, this is a time when a romance with someone at work can be in the cards. But it may be in both of your interests to keep this private for the time being to avoid becoming the object of idle gossip. If you are married, remind yourself of what you have to lose.

Saturday the 17th. Treat yourself to something fashionable for those special nights out. Buy what you like rather than being swayed by someone else. This is a time when children can be growing out of everything they possess. This can be a good time for finding bargains. A friend with older children may have some things to pass on. If a loved one is feeling low this evening, tread carefully.

Sunday the 18th. This can be a stressful day. If you feel your boss or co-worker is being unfair, do not to take too much lying down. Show that you cannot be bullied. A parent can be critical. Tolerance can be your best policy, but you should object if it goes too far. Guard against nursing resentments. Let someone know if you are angry.

Weekly Summary

You Libras who have been busy working hard or playing hard are probably due for some rest this week. And while responsibilities may not let up just when you want them to, do what you can to take it easy. Those of you who are in a position to work at home may find this an ideal time to do so. This is no time to let yourself get overwhelmed with paperwork or unreasonable demands which really can wait. People in high places may be on your side.

The weekend is likely to find you in a much brighter and lighter mood than you have had during the week. Fun and romance cannot take a backseat forever. Those of you who have been making too many sacrifices of your own plans in order to fulfill promises and obligations may not realize how much you have been holding back. Get ready for an exciting Saturday. However, try not to be too outrageous in your choice of leisure activities. Someone on whom you depend may not approve of all the freedom you are likely to allow yourself these days. Be prepared to have to answer for any behavior viewed as irresponsible.

34th Week/August 19–25

Monday the 19th. While you may be reluctant to burden friends with your problems, remind yourself that you would willingly do the same for them. Being at home with small children can be claustrophobic. Make a point of going out for at least part of the day. If you are unemployed, be extra cautious about get-rich-quick schemes; you can end up worse off.

Tuesday the 20th. There is a good chance that your current employer will raise your salary if there is a possibility of losing you. You may be in a stronger position than you realize. Use the phone to go after money that is owed you. A tax bill may be lower than anticipated. This can be a favorable time for mending a broken romance.

Wednesday the 21st. You Libras usually have definite ideas about what you like and do not like. Decorating can be difficult if you and your partner have different tastes; be prepared to compromise. Avoid lending money to friends. They may have the best intentions to pay you back, but they may not be able to honor them. Avoid making vague social arrangements.

Thursday the 22nd. A fellow commuter may strike up a conversation; this can develop into a friendship or even a romance if you are single. The more you can get to know someone, the greater the chances of making a successful choice. This can be a productive day for you Libra writers; you may be able to put the finishing touches to a book with the help of your editor.

Friday the 23rd. With the best will in the world, there are bound to be times when you feel that you do not have enough energy to cope. If you are recently retired, this can be a day when you feel bored or aimless. You may consider finding out about some volunteer work if you think that you need a new challenge or outside interest. A date may be canceled.

Saturday the 24th. If your partner is inclined to leave a lot of the work to you, make a point of asking for a more equal input. This is a day when you should be careful to request rather than demand if you want to make changes at home; otherwise, you run the risk of being accused of bossiness. This can be a good evening for having a dinner party, but one guest may be late.

Sunday the 25th. You may have no choice but to put in some work even on Sunday. This is unlikely to go down well with your partner or other members of your family. Try to meet halfway. This is a day when you may need to ask yourself if you are making too many excuses for someone's lack of effort. Look at the facts rather than just relying on how you feel; you may need to be more demanding.

Weekly Summary

You Libras who are well-heeled enough to be looking for a good investment may want to have a fresh look at the real estate market. Your dream house can be more within your reach than you have ever imagined. Putting money into your home looks advantageous right now. However, shared ownership schemes are probably best avoided.

You Libras who earn your living by mental effort are likely to find yourselves in the midst of dynamic times. If writing is your game, you can be drawn to projects that are more serious or which require more intense research than ever before. A rule of thumb for the time being will be to watch out for ruthless agents. Remember who is working for whom.

This looks like a sensitive weekend, which can best be spent at home. If you who have been under pressure from those people who are supposed to be coming to your support, no wonder you are feeling confused. Everybody needs love and acceptance, including you. These things cannot be demanded, but it may help to let those concerned know how you feel.

35th Week/August 26–September 1

Monday the 26th. In your willingness to be of assistance, make sure that your own jobs do not get pushed to one side. This can be a good time for arranging appointments over the phone. Confirm them by letter. If you are unemployed, you may be offered a temporary position. If you are engaged in sports of any kind, guard against taking unnecessary risks of injury.

Tuesday the 27th. You should find that you have plenty of time to formulate and experiment with new projects. This can be a good day to develop your natural powers of creativity. Art or drama lessons can be particularly successful. For you Libras who are unattached, someone's interest in you may come to your notice. Do be encouraging if the feeling is mutual.

Wednesday the 28th. Attack routine jobs with renewed vigor. There are parts to any job that can be tedious. Make an appointment to see your doctor if you are concerned about your health. You may be suffering from overwork. Make a point of having a restful evening and an early night; catching up on your sleep can be a tonic in itself.

Thursday the 29th. Compatible life-styles can be a good starting point for sharing the same living space successfully. If you are out shopping, this can be a good time for a visit to a music shop; you may be able to add some favorites to your collection. An evening out straight from work can be good fun; you could also run into other friends while you are out.

Friday the 30th. Business meetings can be successful on the whole, but some persistence may be necessary to get your proposals accepted. Guard against being intimidated by someone's overbearing or stern attitude; remind yourself that everyone is human under the tough exterior. Loved ones may feel that they have been neglected. Set this evening aside for them.

Saturday the 31st. Friction at home, either with your partner or another member of your family, can come to a head early in the day. Running away is not going to resolve the problem. Avoid sarcasm. Realize that you may have got hold of the wrong end of the stick; make an effort to listen to the facts. Do not rely on others for entertainment; make your own plans.

Sunday September 1st. Work around the house or garden at a leisurely pace. If there are small children around, be extra vigilant when it comes to watching the cooking area; their curiosity can result in a mishap. This can be a favorable time for tackling jealousy problems within a personal relationship. Realize that this usually stems from insecurity; your partner may simply be in need of some extra reassurance.

Weekly Summary

Those of you who are burning the candle at both ends may need some reminding that life is not only about work. Wednesday's Full Moon can help you to put things in perspective, even if it means taking the day off. You hardworking Libra professionals may be right in wanting to do everything well, down to the last detail. However, do not allow yourself to get so embroiled in professional matters that you lose contact with your own self.

This is an important time, though probably not an easy one for close partnerships. You are entering a cycle where it may be even more difficult to make use of your natural Libra diplomacy. Nobody would argue that self-expression is an integral part of personal freedom. However, this is a time when you are more than likely to upset the apple cart by saying the first thing that pops into your mind. If you find yourself getting deeper and deeper into hot water, especially on Saturday, it may make sense to retreat and be on your own for a while. Those of you who are married or in committed relationships may feel inclined to act out if you feel hemmed in. Try to control any impulses that can be destructive.

36th Week/September 2–8

Monday the 2nd. Guard against aiming too high too soon. By all means apply for a promotion, but be realistic about your chances of getting the job and your ability to manage it successfully. If you are starting a new job on Labor Day, expect a lot of confusion; someone may not have the time to give you the personal attention you need. Pick up as much as you can and do not panic.

Tuesday the 3rd. If you want to return to full-time education as a mature student, this can be a good time for finding out about getting in. Think carefully about entering into a legal battle; you can be letting yourself in for a lot of stress with no guarantee as to the outcome. Make sure you take responsibility for things rather than trying to blame or sue someone else.

Wednesday the 4th. If you seem to be getting nowhere fast, a fresh approach may be needed. Guard against taking other people's assurances too seriously. There is a risk they will forget a promise almost as soon as it is made. This is unlikely to be a good day for long-distance travel; inexplicable delays can leave you feeling uptight. Make sure that luggage is clearly labeled.

Thursday the 5th. A job offer of work should be worth following up, even if it is not exactly what you want to do. It may lead to other things. For you Libra teachers, this can be a good time for securing work abroad, especially if you do not have any family commitments. The chance to live in another country may be too good an opportunity to pass up.

Friday the 6th. If you find that you are being made the scapegoat for someone else's mistakes, it is up to you to clear yourself, even if it means entering a full-scale argument. Guard against handing in your notice in a fit of pique; finding another job may not be as easy as you think. Meeting a deadline may prove impossible. Overtime may be inevitable.

Saturday the 7th. Keep a close eye on small children; they may have a tendency to wander off. Participating in team sports can be fun; the competitive spirit may be stronger than usual, especially if you are playing a return match with a rival team. Try to take defeat graciously if your side loses. Later on, get together with friends and recall stories from the past.

Sunday the 8th. The solution to a work problem can fall into place on its own. This afternoon is likely to be sociable. A lunchtime party can easily run on for the rest of the day. If you are single, there is a good chance of meeting someone new at a social occasion. You may be surprised at how easy the conversation flows. Be sure to exchange telephone numbers.

Weekly Summary

This is an action-packed week, astrologically speaking. If the old adage, as above, so below, holds true for you, look forward to a lot of ups and downs.

Tuesday sees a change that should be welcome for everyone. You Libras can be able to feel confident within yourself, even if there are no real situations or events to justify it. In fact, your challenge may be only in finding ways to channel what can be an abundance of emotional energy. Your ability to be patient, forgiving, and to see things philosophically will come in handy on Wednesday. That is when a new cycle starts which can cause annoying delays and misunderstandings, especially in everyday matters. As a matter of fact, those of you who can delay making a final decision on an important matter will be wise to do so until normal conditions return on the 26th.

As if all this were not enough, another change kicks in on Saturday. This one may help you to work out any difficulties you may be having with friends. You Libras are coming out of a serious cycle which may have had an inhibiting effect on your social life. Look forward to better times ahead.

37th Week/September 9–15

Monday the 9th. Pooling resources and ideas can mean certain jobs get done remarkably quickly. If you are politically active, this should be an excellent day to canvass for the upcoming election. For you business people, now can be a good time for boosting your advertising; a good agency can be worth its weight in gold. Money spent on public relations is likely to repay itself several times over.

Tuesday the 10th. This can be a good time for offering your services to a charitable organization. Administrative skills can be particularly helpful. This can be an excellent time for expanding your social circle. A neighbor may be willing to introduce you to people or to clubs. Personalized stationery can be the perfect gift for a friend who has just bought a new home.

Wednesday the 11th. This is likely to be a busy day. Be careful not to make careless errors in your haste. Back up all work you do on a computer. Teamwork can be essential. Guard against imposing your own ideas too forcefully on others. A shy colleague needs to be encouraged to make his or her own suggestions. If you are going out tonight, leave the car at home.

Thursday the 12th. Your ability to learn from past mistakes can be of great value. Keep yourself informed of the moves of your competitors. This is likely to be a good day for confidential meetings. Someone who has been difficult to get hold of can now be willing to give you undivided attention. If you have a young family, this can be a favorable time for making financial provisions for their future.

Friday the 13th. The best way to ensure that a secret is kept is not to tell anyone, even a best friend. If you keep a personal diary make sure that it is put away in a safe place, even under lock and key. Someone may not be able to resist the temptation to peep if you leave it lying around. You may find it difficult to get along with a close friend's new partner.

Saturday the 14th. This can be a good time for putting your own needs first. Try to spend the day doing exactly what you enjoy; partners are likely to let you have your own way. This can be a good time for shopping for personal accessories. If you are unhappy with your personal appearance, this can be a good time for making changes. A bit of pampering may not go amiss.

Sunday the 15th. A dream can be disturbing; you may realize that you are more deeply affected by something than you thought. If you are having marriage problems, this is unlikely to be a good day for having a showdown with your spouse. Tempers can flare quickly. Think carefully about the real issues.

Weekly Summary

You Libras who are involved in political, social action, or humanitarian groups can look forward to a lively start to the week. Your willingness to tell it like it is can be a real boost, not only to the kindred spirits who share your beliefs, but also to the supporters on whom you are financially dependent. If you can keep your message straightforward and to the point, you should be able to get more appreciation for what it is you are trying to accomplish. Later on in the week, it may become necessary to be especially discreet. Your collective desire to make the world a better place can probably not be furthered in the long run by shock tactics or finger-pointing.

Those of you who have been developing plans and projects to further your own personal goals may want to check into evening classes and weekend courses; they may be starting about now. Pay a visit to your local library or adult education office to see what is on offer. If you can manage to spend some quiet time alone at the time of Thursday's New Moon, use it to take a personal inventory. Get in touch with goals that are still meaningful to you, and disregard the rest. Saturday looks ideal for stepping into action.

38th Week/September 16–22

Monday the 16th. You may hear today that a colleague is leaving for new pastures. You may take it upon yourself to organize a collection for a going-away present, but ask for realistic contributions so that it is affordable for everyone. Be cautious about lending out your personal belongings to a friend; there is a risk that something could be broken or spoiled. Try not to fritter money away this evening.

Tuesday the 17th. This can be a lucky day as far as money is concerned; a tax refund or other money can find its way to you. An older relative may be willing to help out with extra expenses. There may be good news for your partner in regard to a new job. Friends can have a happy occasion to announce, such as a wedding or a christening. Your own love life should be hitting some high notes.

Wednesday the 18th. Public transport can be slower than usual; be prepared to fork out for a cab if you are running late for an important appointment. A certain individual can be a godsend when it comes to lightening your work load or making helpful suggestions. You Libra parents will find this evening a good time for helping children with homework or school projects.

Thursday the 19th. Make a point of not listening to gossip or participating in it. Say only those things that you would be prepared to say to someone's face. If you are away from your place of work, make sure you get your telephone messages; there may be something that will demand your immediate attention. The best way to remember important things is to write a list.

Friday the 20th. Forthcoming changes are unlikely to be clear at the moment. Be patient for the time being.

Some skepticism in your business dealings will stand you in good stead; your feeling that someone is not giving you the whole story is probably justified. Delay signing documents or even making verbal agreements until you are in full possession of the facts.

Saturday the 21st. This can be a good day for catching up on current affairs and finding out more about what is going on in the world. You Libra students will find this a favorable time for doing some reading. You may also need to order some books that are too obscure to be found easily. Steer clear of large gatherings; a heart-to-heart talk with a loved one can be more rewarding.

Sunday the 22nd. Aim for a lazy start to the day; you may feel more energetic later on. If you have children, you may want to plan for something you can do as a family, such as swimming or a team game. Games that can be played at home can also be good fun for both the younger and older generations. If you are unattached, a new romantic opportunity can happen.

Weekly Summary

You Libras can sometimes be generous to a fault. Remember that the people who love you do not feel that way because you shower them with presents. They just do. Before you go out on any excessive spending sprees, think of other ways by which you can show your appreciation and affection. Monday and Tuesday look like good days to turn over a new leaf financially by embarking on a plan to save money. This is probably no time to worry about keeping up with the Joneses. You have your own hopes and dreams to consider. Someone who is older may able to help you put things into perspective.

The activity quotient is likely to pick up steam as the week progresses. Those of you who have a lot of networking to do are advised to be extra cautious about conducting sensitive or confidential conversations on the telephone, or even by letter. Curious eyes and ears are everywhere, and sometimes it is wise not to forget that. Important people may be monitoring your progress from behind the scenes. If you have a choice between moving back your target and loosening up on security, the former option will be better.

39th Week/September 23–29

Monday the 23rd. It may be a struggle to communicate your ideas to others. But inspiration is likely to strike if you stick at it long enough. You Libra parents may find that others in the family have strong views about private or public education. Choose what you feel is best. Be generous to a friend who is too engrossed in a new romance to have much time for you.

Tuesday the 24th. Odd jobs that have been piling up may now have to be dealt with once and for all. But remind yourself how good you will feel once they are out of the way. It may be difficult to stick to your usual routine if you are at home. At least make a start; maybe you can set yourself a time limit. This can be a good time for checking out your telephone bill.

Wednesday the 25th. If you really need to concentrate, find yourself an empty office for a couple of hours. You Libra students can study more effectively in the library than at home. Learning information by heart can be difficult; ask someone to test you so that you can see how much has sunk in. You Libra journalists think twice about publishing a controversial article.

Thursday the 26th. Someone in authority can delegate a significant amount of work to you. You may have to ask the person to be more realistic about the time it will take. News of a crime in your area will make you more mindful of security. You Libra women may consider learning some basic self-defense techniques. A loved one can still be brooding over a quarrel.

Friday the 27th. Meeting people who are in the same line of work can be fun and educational; you can also make some new friends. This can be a favorable time for taking on a partner or making additions to your staff. If you work for a union, you may be able to secure improved terms and conditions for your members. An impromptu night out can be nice.

Saturday the 28th. A new romance can prove to be short-lived; it may not take very long before you realize that there is little to sustain the relationship beyond the initial physical attraction. Try to remind yourself that there is nothing to be gained from staying in a rut. If you have a joint bank account with your partner, this will be a time when you need to know how much each other is spending.

Sunday the 29th. Understand your own psychological makeup before you try to make sense of anybody else's. You may not be in the mood for accepting a social invitation tonight. It is your prerogative to say no; do not allow yourself to be pressured into doing something that is not your cup of tea. But do not try to stop your partner from going off alone; possessive behavior can backfire.

Weekly Summary

You hardworking Libras who are employed by large organizations may be earning reputations as office renegades. While you may have gotten where you are by getting along with others, it may be that you will have to learn to stand up to your own convictions if you want to continue marching along the same road. Your personal vision is bound to be strong enough to counter any challenges from those who may feel threatened by your growth as an individual. Once everything is out in the open, some compromises can probably be struck. Thursday's Full Moon can be the turning point you have been waiting for.

Thursday also marks the end of that irksome cycle that may have been causing chaos in your daily life. Those of you who have had computer breakdowns, car breakdowns, communication breakdowns, or have been feeling as though you are headed for a nervous breakdown can breathe a sigh of relief. Mischievous Mercury has been the culprit. Things may not be back to normal right away, but there should be a gradual easing up by the end of the week.

40th Week/September 30–October 6

Monday the 30th. Hold on to your shopping receipts. There is a chance that something will have to be returned. Ensure that a manufacturer's guarantee is stamped and dated. This can be a good time for putting your financial affairs in order. Take a look at your insurance needs; a policy may need to be updated. Stand by your decisions at work, even in the face of group opposition.

Tuesday October 1st. You Libra students who are starting a new term will find this an exciting day. It is only natural that you will suffer from homesickness at first. Libras in the legal professions will have a demanding day. Guard against taking on new clients before some existing cases are settled. A court case can be a feather in your cap.

Wednesday the 2nd. Overseas business deals can be lucrative in the long term; but there can be many small details to sort out first. Teaching work of all kinds may be hard to find. If you are newly qualified but cannot find a permanent position, it may be worthwhile to take on substitute work. The theater or a concert this evening may be disappointing.

Thursday the 3rd. If a colleague tries to boss you around, bow to his or her experience if it is greater than yours. A pay dispute may still take some time before a satisfactory offer is made and accepted. Guard against a tendency to take a principle too far; you can cut off your nose to spite your face. If you are about to move in with your partner, be prepared for some teething problems.

Friday the 4th. Make sure that you are not carrying the blame for someone else's mistakes. Standing up for yourself can be difficult, but it is important. Avoid wearing a valued piece of jewelry if it has a loose fastening; there is a risk of losing it. Keep a close hold on your personal belongings if you are using public transportation; an overlooked item may never reach the lost and found.

Saturday the 5th. If you have had to bring work home with you this weekend, get it out of the way as soon as possible. This afternoon is likely to be a busy time. If you have young children, you may find the house full of their friends; be tolerant and try to work around them. This evening can be a good time for inviting a close friend over for a meal.

Sunday the 6th. The company of old friends can be enjoyable. You may decide to cook lunch for everyone. If money is short, you will find that others are willing to make a contribution. A new romance can be on the cards with someone who has so far been a friend. This can be a good time for sharing your hopes and dreams for the future.

Weekly Summary

While it could be argued that you Libras are here to explore the experience of being in relationship with others, that does not necessarily mean your individuality should be compromised. Those of you who have been living your lives for other people are bound to be feeling restless this week. Family members especially may make it only too comfortable to remain in the same old patterns. While there is almost sure to be some confusion as far as what to do next, one fact remains. Can it be that you are losing sight of your highest goals and ideals? Do not let that happen.

As far as confusion is concerned, those of you who have been feeling muddled up by dreaminess may start to feel more in control after Sunday's astrological aspects. If you have been subject to emotional overload, it may be wise to find some way to channel all that energy. Making music is one possibility to explore. The purpose here will not be to become a great musician, but just to enjoy the unique pleasure of producing melodies and tones. For those of you who have the time and inclination, some volunteer work may be in order, especially if it will allow you to have contact with people who need help.

41st Week/October 7–13

Monday the 7th. Making a sales presentation to new clients can be nerve-racking at first; but you should find that you soon get into your stride. Aim for an energetic and punchy style if you are called upon to address an audience. If you are going for a promotion at work, you can find yourself in direct competition with a colleague. There is a risk that associates will steal a march on you.

Tuesday the 8th. If you are buying goods through a catalogue, remember that pictures can be misleading. If you are looking for a secondhand car, this is one time when you cannot afford to trust to luck; you can end up with a lemon. Have an expert opinion before you part with your cash. Better still, ask yourself whether you really need a car at all.

Wednesday the 9th. This can be a lucky day for offers of the sort of work you have been hoping for. You will soon be in the ideal position of getting paid for what you love doing. For you Libras who are unattached, this can be a good time for being brave and asking someone out; the person may just be waiting for the green light. If you are recently married, the subject of starting a family is likely to crop up.

Thursday the 10th. Patience is likely to be the key to resolving complicated situations. Trust your instincts when it comes to taking a gamble. If you want to put your house on the market, you should consider advertising privately first; in this way you can cut out the cost of a real estate agent. Your partner may want to make changes to your social agenda for this evening.

Friday the 11th. Exercise can be a real tonic. If you know that you are not fit, this can be a favorable time for new resolutions. At work, a colleague can have a tendency to make a crisis out of a relatively minor problem. Your ability to cope and come to the rescue may result in some professional jealousy; accept the fact that this is the sort of situation you cannot win.

Saturday the 12th. There are some situations that others just have to sort out for themselves. Your advice is likely to be disregarded at the end of the day. If you live in an apartment, you may consider investing in some window boxes. Fresh flowers can brighten up your favorite room. Return invitations are likely to be received. A dinner party can be a romantic occasion.

Sunday the 13th. No amount of fretting will change something that has to wait until tomorrow anyway. If you have recently fallen out with a good friend, now is the time to put matters in perspective. If you are prepared to be honest with yourself, you can realize that you have overreacted. A reconciliation should be a straightforward matter of being the first to phone.

Weekly Summary

Two big changes dominate the astrological influences at work this week. They occur on Wednesday and Thursday respectively, although you may not feel their full effect until Saturday's New Moon.

The first change further reinforces that which has been going on for some time now. Those of you who have always been interested in other people and in offering a kind word whenever possible may be thrown for a loop when this cycle first begins. You Libras are likely to be more focused in your interests and more honest about what you say than you have ever been in your whole lives. There is a danger, however, of letting that get somewhat out of hand. This short cycle can make it difficult to hold your tongue. Try to be aware of the consequences of speaking out of hand. Hurting someone's feelings is never worth it.

Strong energies are at work on Thursday, strong enough to be felt throughout. You creative Libra people who work in any of the performing and visual arts can be headed for a real breakthrough. Be open to any brainstorms that may be brewing inside or around you.

42nd Week/October 14–20

Monday the 14th. Some quick economizing can be called for to avoid an end of the month squeeze. If you have to break a date, trust that real friends will understand. Accidents at home are more likely. A valuable object may get broken by a clumsy visitor. If you do not have insurance, you may consider taking some out.

Tuesday the 15th. Working with children can have especially rewarding moments; you may feel that they make more sense than the adults in your life. In your business dealings, this is a time when you need to guard against doing too much of the talking. You Libra salespeople can walk away without making a deal if you do not really listen to your clients' needs.

Wednesday the 16th. The ability to come up with the goods on time can count for a lot now, so try not to let the grass grow under your feet. If you have old photographs to be restored, take them to an expert. The extra cost should be well worth the results. In a personal relationship, this is a time when you need to put past mistakes or differences behind you.

Thursday the 17th. Dealing with general inquiries can be time-consuming. For you Libra salespeople this can be a successful morning; you may finally get through to the real decision maker at a certain company just when you are about to give up. Friction at home is unlikely to go away if you ignore it. Be prepared to take the bull by the horns; talk a problem through.

Friday the 18th. This can be a favorable time for bulk buying; you can save a considerable amount. If you are at home, you may have the problem of unwanted callers, for instance, door-to-door salespeople or someone wishing to convert you to a religion or political doctrine. Cut the conversation short if you are not interested.

Saturday the 19th. Do not attempt to do any household repair work yourself unless you really know what you are doing. Keep children away from work areas. Do not buy secondhand appliances. It is better to spend more and have the reassurance of the manufacturer's guarantee. This afternoon can be a good time for taking young children to a zoo or amusement park.

Sunday the 20th. A little exercise each day can soon produce results. If you have young children, this can be a good time for teaching them to swim or at least to be confident in the water. A new romance can benefit from spending some time alone; it may be too early to introduce someone to all your friends and family. You need to get to know each other first.

Weekly Summary

Family and domestic issues are likely to loom large on this week's horizon. Whatever your unique situation may be, you are likely to be feeling that you have bitten off more than you can chew on the home front. Those of you who are trying to keep several balls spinning in the air simultaneously will be feeling emotionally exhausted during early hours. If you are in the unpleasant situation of having a partner your family does not approve of or get along with, you may have to go further into the extended family for the support you seek. At times such as these, it can be hard to decide where to put your trust. Nobody ever said it would be easy. However, the time comes eventually when it at least appears that you have to take sides.

You Libras are in the midst of a long cycle that can have an effect on your ability to travel. Those of you who are accustomed to jumping in the car whenever you feel like it may already be experiencing setbacks that compel you not to take traveling for granted. This week, you should be able to come up with some creative means of getting the information and service you need without having to leave your base.

43rd Week/October 21–27

Monday the 21st. Try to regard competition as a healthy challenge rather than to feel threatened by it. If you are working with children, devise activities that use surplus energy in a creative way. Discipline problems can arise if you allow boredom to set in. Do not hesitate to let your employer know of your ambitions; he or she can help you to achieve them.

Tuesday the 22nd. If you suffer from a persistent health problem, this can be a good time for investigating the options offered by the field of alternative medicine. You may be surprised at how quickly you get results. If you are at home, this can be a good time for having a blitz on the housework. Jobs that you would put off may not seem so tedious once you get started.

Wednesday the 23rd. If you are out of work, this is a time when a hospital or hospice may be grateful for some volunteer work. You Libras who are single can have a secret admirer who is too shy to be more obvious; try to spot the signs. A positive new work cycle can be opening up; make sure that you capitalize upon it. Steer clear of jargon when you make a pitch.

Thursday the 24th. There is a risk that your new partner may not live up to your expectations. A cautious start can mean saving yourself a lot of hurt. Be dubious about people who make extravagant promises. Their good intentions are unlikely to come to anything. Working toward a deadline can be stressful. If you have to break a date, let people know early.

Friday the 25th. Meetings of all kinds can be productive now. Stumbling blocks that you have been anticipating are unlikely to arise. This can be a happy time for brothers or sisters. If they have been through separations, they may now be settled with someone new. This can be a good day for finishing written work of any kind that will count toward a qualification.

Saturday the 26th. A couple of stiff letters to clients who owe you money can have the desired effect. If you are taking on new work, be sure to ask for a realistic deposit. If you share a bank account with your partner, this is a day when arguments about money are very likely to crop up. It may be a case of having different priorities when it comes to allocating income.

Sunday the 27th. For you Libra parents, this is a time when children may be pestering you for the latest fad in toys or games. If buying them is beyond your means, try to explain it clearly; it is never too soon for children to learn the value of money. You may find yourself attending a social occasion against your better judgment. If you feel out of your depth, make your excuses and leave.

Weekly Summary

Those of you who are running at full speed these days may need some extra reminders to take good care of yourselves. Somehow or other, you know exactly how to do that, even if you are not entirely aware of it. It has been said that the three most important keys to a healthy body are a good diet, regular exercise, and forgiveness. That should give you food for thought.

The subject of money can be a sticky matter this week. Those of you who are saving up to buy a home or enlarge the one you're in will be wise not to act on every impulse. You Libras who share your financial resources with a partner or family member may have to develop the art of compromise to new heights. Money is a magnet for deep feelings which sometimes are unconscious. If you and your partner find yourselves arguing about it, it probably will be a good idea to read between the lines and listen to what is being said behind the words you hear. The situation may come to a head around Saturday's Full Moon. If it does, try to put your selfish instincts to one side and turn up your compassion. Trust is probably at stake here, and your willingness to take financial risks is based on it.

44th Week/October 28–November 3

Monday the 28th. If you are looking for furniture, this can be a favorable time for attending an auction. There is a good chance of picking up just what you need at a fraction of its regular price. This can be a challenging day for you Libras who work in the caring professions; you may have to put in a longer shift than usual. Counseling can help a personal problem.

Tuesday the 29th. A change of scenery will do you good. You may consider making plans to get away. This can be a productive day for you Libra full-time students. Hours of research can pay off when you finally get to grips with a difficult subject. If you are looking for work abroad, more than one offer can be made; but you may have to leave on short notice.

Wednesday the 30th. If you feel that your partner is holding you back from developing your career, this may be the right time for a serious talk. Try to find out what the real issues are, and ask your partner to meet you halfway. You should be able to reach some workable compromises. This can be a favorable time for buying a new car. A night out can be enjoyable.

Thursday the 31st. If you are interviewing for a job, remember that the key to success may lie in asking pertinent questions of your own. In this way you can show a prospective employer that you are serious about the job. Do not allow yourself to be discriminated against on the basis of family commitments. In business dealings, stick to tried and trusted methods.

Friday November 1st. This can be a good time for securing venture capital; but make sure that you fully understand the terms and conditions. If you are about to go self-employed, you should be able to get financial support from your bank if you can present a clear, well-thought-out proposal. Your main asset may be your confidence and belief in yourself.

Saturday the 2nd. Give as generously as you can when you are approached for a donation to a worthwhile cause. If you are out shopping for clothes, it may be helpful to take along a friend whose taste you trust and whose suggestions can point you in the right direction. If you have a new romantic partner in your life, this can be a time to introduce your love to friends.

Sunday the 3rd. If you are unemployed at the moment, this can be a good time for buying up all the newspapers and scrutinizing the help wanted pages. This can at least give you an idea of the sort of jobs there are on the market. If you want to retrain for a new profession, you need to find out about the costs involved. Someone in the family may be willing to help you out when it comes to fees.

Weekly Summary

Nothing is more creative than falling in love. You Libras are capable of doing it almost at the drop of a hat. It may be good to keep in mind, however, that there is a big difference between being openhearted and being fickle. Likewise, there is no harm in being playful with someone you love or might love. But playing games is bound to get you into deep trouble. You are likely to find yourself in a free-flowing mood as far as matters of the heart are concerned, especially early in the week. Try not to neglect your tried-and-true relationships while you are so keen on exploring and expanding new horizons.

Professional concerns may lead to a more sober mood in the proceedings by Wednesday. Those of you who harbor ambitions to move up are advised to be especially discreet. Keep your secret a secret, especially from partners who may prefer you to remain exactly as and where you are. Doing a bit of confidential research may come in handy when the matter of salaries comes up. Don't push your luck.

45th Week/November 4–10

Monday the 4th. If you are harboring a grievance toward someone, now is the time to get things out into the open. Clear the air, even if it does mean having a full-scale row. You Libra professionals may be suffering from overwork. Be alert to telltale signs of stress, such as headache or short temper. The long-term effects of overstretching yourself can be very serious.

Tuesday the 5th. Whatever your job, this is a time when you can afford to have confidence in your own abilities. Hard-won experience can now come into its own. Remind yourself that knowing your own strengths and weaknesses can mean that it is impossible for others to put you down. Be sure to vote before the polling places close.

Wednesday the 6th. Even complicated tasks have a way of simply falling into place. If you work for a charity, this can be an excellent time for launching an advertising campaign; you are quite likely to capture the sympathy of the public. This is a day when you can be on the receiving end of confidences. Being trusted with intimate concerns can boost your self-esteem.

Thursday the 7th. Do not allow someone else's bad mood to affect you. This can be a good time for taking up a new hobby, especially something that you have never tried your hand at before. Tap into your creative skills, which may have been lying dormant for too long. Do not let others pour cold water on your enthusiasm; you never know what you can do until you try.

Friday the 8th. Be realistic about the time it will take to complete the job at hand. This can be a difficult time when it comes to resolving an ongoing problem with your spouse. You may find that your love has a tendency to be dismissive. Accept that you will have to be persistent if you want to be taken seriously. Resist the temptation to exaggerate to win sympathy.

Saturday the 9th. This may be a good time for increasing your children's weekly pocket money; in this way you can encourage them to save for some things themselves instead of always coming to you. If you are in the process of decorating your home, do not be too hasty when it comes to deciding on color schemes.

Sunday the 10th. Recent efforts to reduce a debt can now be bearing fruit. You may find that you are better off than you have been for a while. There may be an event to celebrate in the family, such as an anniversary or someone's promotion at work. This can be a favorable day for entertaining at home; there may be some surprise guests.

Weekly Summary

You Libras who work in any of the helping professions or who look after elderly family members or friends can benefit from a few words of encouragement. Seeing someone else suffer is always difficult and is bound to bring up painful memories of your own. Before you cause any big scenes, it will probably be helpful to all concerned if you put yourself in the position of the person needing help. Then you can set out on a plan of action. If you can accept things as they are, you can be the greatest help of all. Seeing things in a broad, philosophical framework can make all the difference.

Hold on to your wallet toward the end of the week, especially if you've just been paid. The impulse to spend, spend, spend can be especially hard to resist on Saturday. There is nothing necessarily wrong with that unless you are unconsciously compensating for something else that is bothering you. Sunday's New Moon can help you to see things more clearly and to clarify your values. Once you have that settled, feel free to go shopping for the house or garden.

46th Week/November 11–17

Monday the 11th. If you live in a shared household, this can be a good time for opening a bank account for domestic expenses. Agree on a figure for each person to pay in each month. This afternoon is likely to be busy. If your paperwork is getting out of control, you may consider reorganizing your filing system. Being able to put your hands on a document at a moment's notice can save a lot of time.

Tuesday the 12th. Stop a small problem from becoming a big one by having it put right now. You may find that you are running on a short fuse; little things can annoy you. This may be due to the fact that a personal anxiety is weighing heavily on your mind. Make an extra effort to apologize quickly if you upset someone over something that is clearly not their fault.

Wednesday the 13th. There is more than one way of getting what you want. Allowing yourself to get uptight or frustrated can be counterproductive. Others may keep you waiting around, but this does not mean that you have to hang around indefinitely. Tell people to get back to you when they are really free. It may be wise to confirm business appointments.

Thursday the 14th. This should be a good time for approaching your boss about a raise or some time off. Superiors are likely to be more generous than usual. You Libra salespeople are advised to try to fill next week's diary with appointments rather than to relying on cold calling. Keep a few aces up your sleeve. Do not discuss deals until they are safely in the bag.

Friday the 15th. You may not be firing on all cylinders this morning, but your energy should pick up as the day goes on. Feeling tired can mean that you are prone to being forgetful. Check your calendar for an appointment that may have slipped your mind. If you run into an old friend, arrange to get together when you have more time to chat.

Saturday the 16th. Be careful about whom you get involved with these days. The way that people behave at the outset is often descriptive of their habitual behavior. Keep your eyes wide open. You do not deserve to be taken for granted or treated in a cavalier fashion. An argument with a loved one may be irreparable for the time being. Be patient.

Sunday the 17th. This can be a lucky day as far as money is concerned. For you Libras who are recently separated, this can be the day when you feel that life is looking up again. A new romance can make you thankful that you got out of an unhappy relationship. If you have been putting off starting a family for financial reasons, you may decide to go ahead.

Weekly Summary

You Libras who are getting more serious about your current relationship may feel ready to take the plunge and marry. If that is your situation, do not make the mistake some people make by keeping secrets from one another. While it might be true that romance depends on having at least a bit of mystery, that would not justify holding back thoughts or ideas from your prospective spouse. Everyone has skeletons in the closet. However, the sooner they come out, the sooner we can all begin to accept one another as we are. As far as relationships are concerned, you Libras are probably learning a great deal this year. If your partner is not one to open up, it is up to you to initiate honest conversations about issues to be addressed.

Those of you with children in your care are likely to become more interested in your child's education this week. If your child has a learning difficulty or some other problem at school, set aside time on the weekend to talk things over and see for yourself what is going on. When children know they are taken seriously, they are more likely to apply themselves.

47th Week/November 18–24

Monday the 18th. Tackling tedious tasks is probably the last thing you feel like doing; you may have to dig into your resources of self-discipline. You cannot afford to put off routine health checkups. A recurring headache can be a sign of eye strain. Unkind gossip about someone you know well can come to your ears; it is up to you to defend the person.

Tuesday the 19th. An obvious answer has been staring you in the face all this time. If you have spare time during the day, this can be a good time for joining a fitness class, such as aerobics or yoga. The company of others can be the best way to keep yourself motivated. If money is short, this can be a good time for making your own clothes or restyling old items.

Wednesday the 20th. Be clear when it comes to giving instructions to others. Delays can arise when you realize that someone has not understood what you wanted. Do not resort to underhand tactics or tempting shortcuts; your professional reputation may be at stake. Accept the fact that a certain transaction will take as long as it takes.

Thursday the 21st. If you are having work done at home, the place may begin to resemble a building site; it can take longer to finish than was originally estimated. You will just have to keep reminding yourself that all the mess and inconvenience will be worth it in the end. Your partner may have itchy feet at the moment; trust your dear one to go off alone.

Friday the 22nd. Some nagging worry may be taking the edge off your enjoyment of a new romance. You are likely to let it grow out of proportion if you do not bring it out into the open. Other people can be more receptive than you imagine. If you are out shopping with small children in tow, make sure that you keep them close by; there is a risk of having to pay for something they break.

Saturday the 23rd. If you usually leave your holiday shopping to the last minute, you should consider doing things a bit differently this year. If you have been saving for something special, this is a time when you can achieve your goal. This can be a propitious day for redecorating a lackluster room. You single Libras can find yourself being talked into a blind date; be courageous and give it a shot.

Sunday the 24th. The day is likely to start off at a relaxed pace. You may be in the mood for spending some time on your own, just doing nothing in particular. An unexpected invitation to join friends on a trip out of town can be too good an opportunity to pass up. For you Libra sports people, there is a good chance that you will score a convincing victory.

Weekly Summary

As the end of the year looms closer on the horizon, those of you who work in offices may be under increasing pressure to complete various projects. In your desire to meet your commitments and earn your stripes, try not to take on more tasks than you can realistically manage at any one given time. The Monday blues shouldn't last much longer than that, so be patient if someone tries to burden you with a mountain of paperwork.

Those of you who are getting ready to make some long-term investment decisions can look forward to what looks like a healthy new financial cycle which gets underway on Saturday. While you Libras are probably learning to trust your instincts to a greater extent than you have in the past, that does not mean it is wise to take any outrageous risks. The weekend appears to be a good time to read up on the current state of the market so that you can make more reasonable decisions. Hi-tech, computer, or electronic stocks may be too unstable to touch right now. Real estate may be a better bet, providing you can get a trustworthy lead on a good property.

48th Week/November 25–December 1

Monday the 25th. A superior on the warpath can be tricky to handle. But be prepared to take the rap for mistakes that you know you are responsible for. Legal matters can be demanding. An adversary may be only too quick to stoop to underhand tactics, such as fabricating evidence; keep your wits about you. A new overseas business connection can prove to be more trouble than it is worth.

Tuesday the 26th. If you are thinking of spending Christmas away from home this year, this can be a good time for collecting travel brochures. You Libra students will find this a favorable day to bring some written work to a conclusion. You are more likely to retain information that you gather. This can be a good time for all endeavors aimed at self-improvement.

Wednesday the 27th. You may make a dramatic improvement in your current salary by looking elsewhere. Good references can be essential when it comes to beating the opposition. You Libra business people will find this an excellent time for entertaining clients. A formal occasion this evening can be enjoyable and productive.

Thursday the 28th. If you are newly self-employed, you may be recognizing the importance of getting your name established. Word-of-mouth advertising can be helpful. Make use of it at social gatherings you attend this Thanksgiving Day. In your involvement with your own work do not forget to take an interest in what your partner does for a living; he or she may be feeling undervalued.

Friday the 29th. Teamwork of all kinds should be successful on the whole. Do not be afraid to ditch ideas or policies that are clearly not working. There is nothing to be gained from sticking to conventional methods just for the sake of it. A romance with someone who has been a friend for a while can be tempting; but it may not be a change for the better.

Saturday the 30th. You may be feeling frustrated by a lack of money at the moment; it seems as if everything you want to do costs too much. Guard against attaching too much importance to material things. For the time being, you will get more pleasure from developing your personal relationships. Spend the evening with those you care for and who care for you.

Sunday December 1st. This can be a time when meeting new people can be enjoyable. Friendships made at this time are likely to stand the test of time. Conversation can soon develop into good-natured debate over the political or social issues of the day; you may find yourself revising your own ideas when someone presents a convincing case for the opposite view.

Weekly Summary

Those of you who are hoping to make further progress in your career will have some opportunities to look forward to this week. Discussions about future business strategy are more likely to go in your direction if they are conducted behind closed doors. If you play your cards right, you will be able to negotiate a solid raise. Wednesday looks good for financial negotiations. However, avoid making promises you may not be able to keep.

While you Libras may not like to draw fixed boundaries in any relationship, it may make sense to begin now. It has been said thousands of times how dangerous and disappointing it can be to mix business and friendship. Saturday looks like an especially bad day to borrow or lend money if it involves a friend. Those of you who go on shopping expeditions probably are most likely to break this simple rule. If you want to protect yourselves from potential resentment, follow the old adage: neither a borrower nor a lender be. Otherwise, both Friday and the weekend look ideal for getting together with friends. They are likely to take a real interest in your personal plans, and can even offer insights into any partnership difficulties.

49th Week/December 2–8

Monday the 2nd. You Libra business people should double-check that you have all the necessary information with you for appointments out of the office. Appearing to be unprepared can lose you a client's good regard. This can be a good time for having a private telephone line put through to your office. Check your personal diary; a birthday or anniversary may have slipped your mind.

Tuesday the 3rd. Other people's advice or help can clutter your mind and confuse the real issues. Your hunches are likely to be correct; have the confidence to act on them. Do not let what other people think be the reason for holding back from pursuing a personal goal. Someone may make you an offer that you should seriously consider over the next few days.

Wednesday the 4th. Refuse to accept vague or incomplete answers to your proposals. You may feel that a personal relationship is going nowhere. While there is a time for being patient, there also comes a time when you want some reassurances about the future. If you suspect that this commitment will never be forthcoming, maybe you should be looking elsewhere.

Thursday the 5th. You should have every reason to feel optimistic about life generally. Your charm and enthusiasm can rub off on others. For you Libras who write for a living, this can be a day for lucky breaks. There is a chance of being granted an interview with a well-known person, such as a film celebrity or a politician. If you work as a free-lancer, you may be able to secure a lucrative book deal.

Friday the 6th. Avoid being manipulative in order to get your way. You are far more likely to be heeded if you make straightforward requests. You Libras often have a struggle when it comes to making a decision and sticking to it. Now this struggle can cause you more anxiety than usual; all you can do is to try to follow your gut instinct. Hanukkah observances for some of you will take your thoughts away from anxieties.

Saturday the 7th. This can be an excellent day for holiday shopping, especially if you can make an early start. Make a point of asking your friends or family what they would like; then you will not make the wrong choice, and shopping will be much quicker. This evening can be a good time for accepting an invitation to a dinner party; conversation should be interesting.

Sunday the 8th. Weekend guests can be a genuine pleasure to have around. Mixing with others can actually improve the quality of your relationship with your partner. A relative or close friend can have some sound advice about investing money. This can be a good time for getting out into the countryside and taking nature shots. Add to the family photo album.

Weekly Summary

This is probably turning out to be an important year, although perhaps not an easy one, for relationships. Those of you who are working hard at overcoming your resistance to being close, or whatever other fears or insecurities you may have, can look forward to what should be a positive shift this week. This should be especially good news if you have felt that you and your partner have been taking two steps back for every step forward. You can probably expect things to remain serious, especially on Tuesday. However, slow and steady progress can now be made.

You Libras who are house hunting may find the property you are looking for before the year is out. The weekend looks good for checking out what is new on the market, or even signing a letter of intent to buy.

Before you finalize anything, however, make sure you have a thorough check of all the hidden places inside, above, and below your house. Trouble can be lurking where you least expect it. If this is your first purchase, you should get advice on all the hidden costs, which can be quite substantial. Those of you who are happy where you are may want to spend any extra cash you have on beautifying or enlarging your home.

50th Week/December 9–15

Monday the 9th. This can be a good time for boosting your advertising. You Libra office workers can have fun putting up some decorations. If your work involves serving the general public, this is a day when you are likely to earn a substantial sum in gratuities. You Libras who are weight-conscious will find this a favorable time for starting a diet.

Tuesday the 10th. Waiting for others to get back to you on a business deal can be nerve-racking; but if it is now out of your hands, all you can do is to keep busy with other things. If your car is acting up, get to a garage and have the problem checked out. A family conference can be a sensitive occasion; try to avoid falling out with a brother or sister.

Wednesday the 11th. Someone you no longer want to see can be trying to reestablish contact; realize that you do not have to respond. Friction between you and a loved one is more likely to result in a frosty silence than in an argument. It may be best to leave things this way for the time being rather than to try to force a reconciliation. Invitations need to be answered.

Thursday the 12th. If you have been unemployed for a while, this can be a good time for securing seasonal work. It can be lucrative just when you need extra cash. A bonus from work may be more than anticipated. Check with your partner before you bring guests home this evening; a meal may have been planned just for family or arrangements made to go out.

Friday the 13th. The pressure of work can keep you from attending too many events just for pleasure. You married Libras may need to make an effort to avoid someone's romantic overtures; enjoy being flattered. If you are single, you are likely to meet someone new. You can get to know someone surprisingly quickly if you act naturally and be yourself; abandon any airs.

Saturday the 14th. Keep an eye out for unusual gifts; be inventive when it comes to choosing stocking-fillers. The excitement of young children can rub off on you. A pantomime can be a fun occasion for children and adults. Someone with whom you have not been in contact since last year will probably appreciate an update on your life. There may be a choice of social events this evening.

Sunday the 15th. Make sure your home is not an easy target for burglars. If you are planning to be away, this can be a good time for making provision for household pets. The health of a loved one can be a cause for concern. You may have to abandon your own social arrangements to care for the person. You may benefit from relaxing at home and going to bed early.

Weekly Summary

As the end of 1996 comes more clearly into view, you Libras may be getting anxious about tying up any number of loose ends. Those of you who are involved in sales or who serve as agents for other enterprises can have an especially productive start to the week. However, this is a time when it will be wise to look beneath the surface. Power struggles may be going on behind the scenes and can affect your future.

Friday and Saturday look like the best days for romance. Those of you who are single can unexpectedly meet someone interesting, perhaps through a relative or a neighbor. Whether you decide to commit yourself or just enjoy a serious fling, opportunities to learn more about love can come your way at just about any time and any place. The people you meet now are likely to be more artistic, creative, and probably less conventional than those who have been in your circle in the past. Whatever obstacles you have had to contend with to learn the joy of living, you are now in a cycle where you can break through them.

51st Week/December 16–22

Monday the 16th. Colleagues can be distracting, but listen carefully when they offer you advice from the benefit of their own experience. You will come out the wiser. Part-time or temporary work can be easier to come by now; take the initiative and ask around. This can be a good evening for socializing with friends from work; you gather useful background information.

Tuesday the 17th. Make sure you keep records up to date for someone who is away; you probably cannot afford to rely on your memory. This can be a favorable time for putting a casual romance onto a firmer footing; knowing exactly where you stand can make you feel much more relaxed. Babysitting arrangements for the festive season can be confirmed now.

Wednesday the 18th. You can be making a lot of work for yourself by taking something too seriously. Try not to spend too long on one task; enlist the help of a friend or colleague for a matter that has you baffled. Disagreements do not have to develop into arguments. Everyone is entitled to a personal point of view. Someone who knows how to make you laugh may be just what you need at the moment.

Thursday the 19th. If you feel that a certain individual is not to be trusted, be careful. Confide only in those who have your best interests at heart. A romance can be going through a difficult time. Having to accept the fact that someone is not falling in love with you can be painful, but the truth has to be better than self-deception in the long run. Seek those who value you.

Friday the 20th. If this is your last working day before the holiday break, make sure that you leave your desk in order; tie up any loose ends of work projects. Your partner can be lucky with money. This may come in the shape of a generous bonus from work. This evening lends itself to a quiet meal with a loved one.

Saturday the 21st. If you are spending the holidays at home, this can be a good day for planning menus for the festive period. If you are expecting guests, do not forget to check if you need to supply a vegetarian option. Make sure that you have paid any outstanding household bills; one may have been overlooked. Some final shopping can take up most of the afternoon.

Sunday the 22nd. This is unlikely to be a good time for sitting around at home. Take yourself off to a museum or exhibit if you enjoy cultural activities, but check opening and closing times before you set off in order to avoid disappointment. If you are planning a trip to the movies later on, book your tickets in advance. If you are missing someone, give the person a call.

Weekly Summary

The astrological weather this week looks conducive to slowing down and giving yourself some time to think about the past as well as the future. Those of you who have a lot of running around to do in preparation for the holidays will probably do well to get as many errands out of the way in the beginning of the week as you can. By Thursday afternoon, a more serious mood is bound to permeate the atmosphere, inviting you to be among people who are comfortable and familiar and where you feel accepted exactly as you are. If that means family for you, make it a point to be together. If you have your mind on relationships of a more romantic nature, just make sure you take them seriously. This is not necessarily a lighthearted week, and attempts to make it so can create problems.

You Libras have probably been through a fair share of challenges and bright times over the course of the past 12 months. As 1997 is just around the corner, you are likely to find a buildup of excitement about the possibilities that lie ahead. Sunday looks like an ideal day to reconnect with your highest ideals and see whether you can get closer to your goal.

52nd Week/December 23–31

Monday the 23rd. If you are at work today, chatting with colleagues and catching up with odd jobs can be enjoyable. Make the most of not having to work under pressure. You Libras who are at home may want to put your feet up this afternoon. If you are looking for last-minute gifts, you should find bargains for someone who has an unusual interest or hobby.

Tuesday the 24th. Certain decisions can fall to you simply because there is no one else around. Do not be afraid to use your own judgment; but delay any matters that you feel unsure about handling on your own. On the domestic front, life can be just as frantic; you may think of all sorts of odds and ends that you forgot to buy. A carol service can be magical.

Wednesday the 25th. Merry Christmas!   If you have a large household, the holiday can be a chaotic and noisy affair; turn a blind eye to the mess and throw yourself into the spirit of things. Do not forget to show your appreciation for a certain gift if you know that a loved one went to a lot of trouble to find it. Younger children probably need supervision with new toys.

Thursday the 26th. This can be a lazy morning, but there may still be a lot of clearing up to do from yesterday. This afternoon should be a more sociable time. Friends may drop by, or you may be invited out to a party. A loved one who has serious decisions to make may want to consult you. Being a good listener will be more important than actually giving advice.

Friday the 27th. Enjoy your popularity. Long-standing hostility between you and a family member has probably gone on too long; make an effort to bury the hatchet. This can be a favorable time for lending support to public events in your neighborhood which are aimed at raising money for charity. Look in on neighbors if they have spent a lot of the holiday alone.

Saturday the 28th. Friends who have been away may be eager to meet; you may consider inviting them over for an informal meal later on. This can be a good time for thinking about your own aims and goals for the future. A dream does not have to stay a dream; it is up to you to make necessary changes so that you can work toward what you really want to do.

Sunday the 29th. If socializing is becoming more of a strain than a pleasure, this can be a good day for enjoying your own company. Do not hesitate to pull out of social arrangements if you are not in the mood. It may be too late to repair a broken romance; there may be too much pain or anger to see your way clear to forgiving. Confiding your feelings to paper can unclutter your mind.

Monday the 30th. You Libra professionals will find this a good time for making plans for the year ahead. But do not bring these up for general discussion just yet. If you are unemployed, an employment agency can have you back to work in the new year. For you Libra students, the day favors quiet reading or research. A relationship problem can be resolved through calm discussion.

Tuesday the 31st. If you are entertaining at home, prepare well in advance to have more time for getting yourself ready. Spare some time to think about the resolutions you want to make for the coming year. Do not be afraid to set ambitious goals. You may favor an intimate gathering at home this evening. Parties can be fun as long as you are in the company of a loved one when the clock strikes twelve.

Weekly Summary

This can be one of those exceedingly hectic holiday periods. That old scouting advice to be prepared will serve you well. At what may be one of the most inopportune times, mischievous Mercury reaches into its bag of tricks on Monday. It comes up with a movement that can cause general chaos for those of you who are planning any kind of holiday travel. While flying is not necessarily going to be a problem, getting to and from the airport can be. Those of you who are using any form of short-run transportation, be it taxi, bus, train or, even your own car, are advised to allow time for delays, breakdowns, or traffic jams.

If you are spending the holiday with family members whom you have not seen for a long time, you will probably get along better if you can just be yourself. This is an ideal time to forgive and forget old wounds and old battles. Try to concentrate on what brings you together rather than what sets you apart. This is probably no time to hide behind your professional achievements or to pull rank on family members who have not done so well. In the process, a miracle can occur; you find yourself making friends with your family.

DAILY FORECASTS:
JULY–DECEMBER 1995

Saturday July 1st. Today will be favorable for affairs of the heart. You can enjoy a musical show or other gathering. A visit to an art gallery or museum can be of interest. Travel to some beautiful place can be inspiring to those who enjoy writing and painting.

Sunday the 2nd. Your health may become a bit of a problem. Allergy sufferers can feel quite uncomfortable. Stock up on medicine. If you have been overdoing the social scene, you may be paying a price for it now. Some of you may have problems with spiritual ideals.

Monday the 3rd. This can be a time to stay in bed if you are running a temperature. One way and another, you seem to have problems with traveling. A car may be giving you trouble. Letters from abroad can make you angry or excited. Take care what you say to a teacher.

Tuesday the 4th. Do not indulge too much in Independence Day festivities. You may need to be a bit more abstemious than usual. In fact, a journey you have planned to see relatives is likely to be canceled for lack of funds or a problem with your health.

Wednesday the 5th. You are likely to continue feeling ill at ease. You may find relations with a superior difficult now. In fact, there can be a struggle inside you over duty and work and your own plans and interests. Figure out where you want to be.

Thursday the 6th. This will be a far better day for communications, especially with relatives who live at a distance. This morning can see you attempting to sort out some sort of muddle at home. A job you have been doing behind the scenes is paying off nicely.

Friday the 7th. You can try approaching a boss about a raise in pay. But be sure that you have all your facts straight first, as communication seems to be a problem. Journeys today can be both costly and frustrating. A relative or sibling can give you depressing news.

Saturday the 8th. You are likely to astonish both yourself and others with your willpower. This will be a good day for really getting down to things with vigor and vitality. Clearing up a lot of unfinished tasks can free your mind from previous worries. Sort out bills.

Sunday the 9th. This will be an auspicious day for social meetings in the neighborhood. Communications with brothers and sisters should be cheerful and openhearted. Old differences can now be patched up.

Monday the 10th. Today can be difficult. You may feel as if you are getting nowhere no matter how hard you try. Travel and communications are likely to be full of delays and obstacles. Try not to let it get you down.

Tuesday the 11th. After yesterday, you can be excused for wanting a day off at home. In fact, you may feel wiped out and simply want to laze about. Relaxing and listening to beautiful music can work wonders.

Wednesday the 12th. You can run into some problems with a boss; you do not see eye-to-eye over certain issues. A conflict between the desire to be at home or at work is strong. You can feel genuinely ill or simply in a mood for a bit of escapism. See a doctor.

Thursday the 13th. Your optimism has returned and positive attitudes pull you back out of the doldrums. A lover can make your day by sending a letter or phoning. Children's education should be a source of hope and pleasure. A feeling of freedom makes you glad.

Friday the 14th. Do not let a lover manipulate you emotionally. Your feelings can be intense. You may suffer from pangs of jealousy and suspicion. Or you may be the victim of another's hate and jealousy. Children can try to coerce you into giving them money. They can upset you by being rude.

Saturday the 15th. Take great care of what is said if you are at work. Repeating gossip or exaggerating stories can get you into a scrape. On the other hand, you may be drawn into helping out by listening to another person's troubles. You meet a most attractive stranger.

Sunday the 16th. Take care not to delude yourself about an influential person whom you idealize. Your idol may be far less romantic than you think. It will be better to be realistic about what that person can do for you. A lot may be promised over future career aims. But through hard work you achieve your ambitions.

Monday the 17th. Partnerships, whether personal or business ones, are highly favored. A superior can reward your efforts. You may even have a promotion. This may entail extra work, but it will be worth it in the long run. It is certainly worth the prestige and power it can give you. Legal matters go well.

Tuesday the 18th. Loving words to a partner may be misinterpreted. Arranging a money deal with others can prove tricky. Someone may be holding on rather tightly to necessary funds. You can enjoy a day with a loved one at an art gallery or on a country outing.

Wednesday the 19th. A partner can give you a bit of a shock. Surprising family news may put you out a good deal. But it is likely to pass quickly enough. A piece of machinery can let you down at home or at work. Try to be diplomatic when dealing with a superior.

Thursday the 20th. This can be a time when you will be able to shine in your chosen field. For those in the public eye, fame or notoriety, depending on which you prefer, may be yours. Your personal bank balance can be looking quite healthy just now. In fact, you feel rich. Love and money are most on your mind.

Friday the 21st. Successful corporate money deals can make your name now. Your imagination and original approach pay off. This will be quite a day for those who are in the writing or journalistic professions. Expect to stir up some ripples in the pond, though.

Saturday the 22nd. Do not let yourself get too optimistic and carried away with all your successes. This may lead you into being careless and starting to make serious mistakes. Take everything in good measure and with a pinch of salt. Do not believe everything.

Sunday the 23rd. You can draw up some practical and sensible agreements with others now. The legal and official side of things must be properly sorted out this week. Your ability to be rational and hardheaded will stand you in good stead. Dealing with older relatives can be a chore. But their stories are interesting.

Monday the 24th. Angry scenes at work are most demanding of your patience and time. You should be feeling very energetic just now. This could lead to an increase in sports activities. If so, take care not to be careless or impulsive, as this may lead to an injury. A sacrifice may have to be made for a loved one.

Tuesday the 25th. An old flame may come back into your life. Your workaday affairs should tick over fairly quietly for a change. Take enough time to create a pleasant working atmosphere. Your advice, on love or money matters, will be most helpful.

Wednesday the 26th. Confusion that arises at home can really disrupt your working day. However, bringing a practical and sensible approach to the situation can help to clear up the muddle. You can do well with money matters for the everyday running of things.

Thursday the 27th. You will feel at your best just now. A pleasant friendship will be very important to you. There can be a fresh start with a group of people that you like. Meeting for discussions can be most fruitful. It is possible that you will lead such a group.

Friday the 28th. Your ability to express yourself positively means that you may be asked to lead a humanitarian or philosophic group. Meeting a famous or influential person can really make a social outing special. An unusual person you meet at work may become a lover. But do not expect it to be more than a fling.

Saturday the 29th. This morning can be rather demanding. You can feel disturbed to find that your money situation has suddenly become very depleted. Large bills for repairs, reconstruction, or heavy tax demands can set you back. Do not act carelessly.

Sunday the 30th. Today indicates contemplation of a spiritual kind. Some of you may enjoy some sort of physical activity, such as walking or climbing. Games of mental skill also will appeal, as will competitions and quizzes. If you are alone, pursue a hobby. If not, your warmth and cheerfulness will ensure good relations.

Monday the 31st. Take disappointments and difficulties in your stride now. Your routine is sure to be messed up by a family situation this morning. This may be due to the need for some sort of repairs. You may need all the patience you can muster to deal with a work colleague. Try not to become too negative.

Tuesday August 1st. You will feel very vigorous and lively. Your mind should be fairly racing with fresh ideas and plans for the future. A group of people with whom you are involved may look to you for guidance.

Wednesday the 2nd. You may feel unsure of a family situation. However, you gain some insight by having a positive discussion with a loved one. You are sure to receive a lot of kindness and consideration from a friend. Your social life will be hectic but fun.

Thursday the 3rd. This may be a day of reckoning for finances. An important person you have admired from afar may now become a friend. Artistic people may try to involve you in their activities. While this can benefit you, it will bring additional expenses.

Friday the 4th. It may be best to postpone signing a corporate deal for a while. It may need some time to sort out certain problems with red tape. In fact, you need to be fully aware of all the details involved.

Saturday the 5th. You have a very busy day. Your relations with a sibling should be good at present. A group you belong to is likely to put on some sort of musical performance. You can take a leading role.

Sunday the 6th. You can feel rather low-spirited just now. Having a good talk with a neighborhood friend can cheer you up. You may experience some sort of delay or frustration while traveling around your area. This can to be a good day for enjoying sports.

Monday the 7th. If you are having some urgent repairs done at home, it will be a good idea to be around to supervise things. All should go well, although you may be a bit staggered at the cost of it all. Friends may pay back old debts now and make you feel richer.

Tuesday the 8th. You can work hard to create your ideal home now. An older person may need your care and sympathy. A parent may be due to come out of a hospital. Co-workers can be surprisingly sensitive and understanding of difficult situations. Take care about revealing financial secrets to a friend or group.

Wednesday the 9th. Today will be excellent for staging local entertainment. The local countryside can prove more interesting than you imagine. You may enjoy a tour of the district by car, especially if this involves children. This can be a good time for making speeches.

Thursday the 10th. This can be a difficult time in your love life. A feeling that your pride is at stake will make you and a loved one fall out over some silly notion. You may not be sure what you want to have together. Money may be a problem also. A friendship may become involved, but this may not be for the best.

Friday the 11th. Something someone says at work can stir up intrigue. There is a need to be more discreet and tactful just now. If you are involved in certain agreements, take care to read the small print. Carelessness can lead to some errors in judgment. A relative or a neighbor may be unwell and need your helpful care.

Saturday the 12th. This can be a useful and productive day to handle correspondence and phone calls. Take care when talking about an illness with a neighbor, who may get very upset or imagine the worst. You can be very cheerful and quite elated today.

Sunday the 13th. You may try to impose certain changes on the family way of life. A restlessness may make it hard to settle down. Relationships with a partner can be cheerful later. Those who are spiritually inclined may meet a person whose words are moving.

Monday the 14th. You are in a reckless and impatient mood. Take care in strenuous physical activity. Your excited and impulsive state of mind may lead you to begin a new relationship you will later regret. A partner may vent anger on you. Beware of making enemies through hot, hasty words.

Tuesday the 15th. Partners and friends should mix well now. You may find yourself taking some leading role in a group situation. Your confidence and pride seem to stand you in good stead just now. Unfortunately a family situation may crop up to disrupt your plans.

Wednesday the 16th. Discussing your joint money situation is likely to clear up a few hidden details. Points you may have missed in the fine print of some agreement can be made more clear by rereading the documents involved. A messenger may bring good news.

Thursday the 17th. This will be a good time for building up confidence and a foundation to any enterprise you are currently engaged in. This can be a favorable day for seeing certain deeply felt ideals coming to some sort of fruition. You may at last receive the funds to go ahead with a charitable home or hospital project.

Friday the 18th. Travel over long or short distances is favored. Carelessness over papers or documents can mean a lot of hassle. However, your luck may just about pull you through a tricky situation. Lawyers can appear most untrustworthy. You can experience a loss of faith or just feel as if you have no one to turn to.

Saturday the 19th. You can find difficulty in getting a neighbor to understand a request. This may be due to language barriers. Call on a lawyer or a spiritual leader to explain something to you. Do not get too carried away with grandiose schemes.

Sunday the 20th. Problems with distant business connections can set back your plans. You may have a disagreement with a spiritual leader over some philosophical issue. But it is sure to end on an amicable note. Attempts to go on any long journeys can be frustrated. However, you find that money always talks.

Monday the 21st. Workaday life may appear to be uneventful at first. But an encounter with a powerful individual may completely change your life. In fact your values can be overturned. Take great care to avoid any dangerous or criminal influences in any way.

Tuesday the 22nd. Be careful dealing with any sharp objects or machinery at work. Too many company dinners can affect your digestive system. However, this will be a good day for serious discussions. Various official or legal details can be sorted out.

Wednesday the 23rd. A meeting of a philosophical or academic group will be interesting. Discussions broaden the mind. You may take an interest in legal or ecology issues. Any secret discussions or plans can go well but may meet resistance from official sources. Things still need to be kept under wraps.

Thursday the 24th. Meetings with communal friends or groups should be undemanding. This is a good day for buying stock for warehouses. Hopes and plans for the future come and go, but you will barely consider them. There may be a lull in social activities.

Friday the 25th. A group of people may try to pressure you into taking on a financial job. If you don't want to do it, you need to withstand their manipulative tactics. Later in the day you can make a fresh start on private plans and any activities that need some peace and quiet. Secret meetings may lead to romance for some.

Saturday the 26th. Do not overdo the strong and silent bit now. You seem to be in the mood to keep your opinions to yourself. Perhaps you have had too many rebuffs. Writers can enjoy getting on with their work. But you may exhaust yourself in enthusiasm.

Sunday the 27th. A serious discussion with an older person can help you understand a money problem. In fact, that person may help you transform your way of dealing with finances. Change some things at home. In creating an ideal home, this can be a day of progress.

Monday the 28th. Do not overdo the romantic bit. You may find yourself in a somewhat compromising situation if you are not careful. However, that may be just where you want to be. If so, this can be a day for fun, leisure, and interesting discussions with partners.

Tuesday the 29th. You may be feeling physically fit and lively; take care lest you burn yourself out by sudden fits of activity. Also rashness and impulsiveness may lead to injuries and sprains. Confusing situations at home may make you feel angry. But you find it hard to express what you feel, as others seem vulnerable.

Wednesday the 30th. You may tend to be a bit excessive in what you have to say. If you are traveling in the local area, you will find this a very busy, if not slightly manic, day. However, you seem very much at ease and able to cope with anything. A secret meeting with an important person may make your day.

Thursday the 31st. This will be a splendid time for getting down to some careful and constructive work. Your disciplined and sensible attitude can help you to sort out any recent money difficulties. Older people can be sympathetic about your needs and can even make a loan. Their wise advice will be of value.

Friday September 1st. Spend the morning seeing to any money matters that may need clearing up. You should get a fresh perspective on finances and a more original way of dealing with them. Some of you may be lucky enough to receive a tax rebate or an inheritance. The afternoon will be good for enrolling in courses.

Saturday the 2nd. You will find it hard to keep your mind from dwelling on thoughts of love. Planning clandestine meetings may keep some of you from paying attention to your work. Others may be more concerned over money matters. Rushing can cause accidents.

Sunday the 3rd. Your liveliness will keep you on the move. Visits to neighbors and relatives, window-shopping, writing letters, and gossiping are going to keep you pretty busy. Teachers can revise study plans and course work for a new term. Students can buy needed supplies. Communications are favored.

Monday the 4th. This is likely to be a most enjoyable Labor Day whether you spend it at work or at home. A beloved parent can be of great service to the family. Relationships with a boss should be most amicable. A possibility of romance is in the cards.

Tuesday the 5th. Your strong desire to be independent may shock the family. You do seem inclined to do things your own way of late. This can lead to trouble if you carry it too far. Others are sure to compete or challenge you. Be careful about accidents in the home.

Wednesday the 6th. Creative writing will now be rewarding and successful. You can express yourself uniquely, making what you say a positive expression of your own way of thought. Help children with school work. You seem to be buzzing with ideas. This can help in communications. Personal plans can be achieved.

Thursday the 7th. There is a danger of compulsive desires taking you over today. These can lead you into a relationship that you may later regret. You are likely to be in a lively and merry mood. Others are sure to find your presence and personality most attractive. This will be a good day for sports and entertainment.

Friday the 8th. You can be unrealistic in your expectations of a current working situation. Others may let you down over some minor but important detail. Feeling out of sorts or ill at ease can make this an uncomfortable day. Some of you Libra people may even be really sick and need to check in with a doctor.

Saturday the 9th. You can spend a good deal more than you intend, especially on furnishings for the home. An older person may need considerable personal attention at present. Although you find your duties difficult, you can be of great value to the community.

Sunday the 10th. A partner can really help your mind to expand with new ideas. These may be about spiritual issues. Feelings of optimism and cheerfulness help make relationships happy. A romance that started at work may turn out to be quite ideal. Your compassion and loving care can have a very helpful effect.

Monday the 11th. This can be a confusing day for a partnership issue. You will find that no matter how hard you try, you are going to be misunderstood. A sudden revelation about a mate may not be to your liking. Be wary of promises made by business partners.

Tuesday the 12th. You need to give a lot of thought to your joint funds now. Company finances may be in need of sorting out rather quickly. Impulsive spending seems to be causing problems at the moment. You may feel driven by a need to make more money.

Wednesday the 13th. Seeing an influential person may mean some sort of promotion for you today. Extra responsibility will give you a lot more confidence in your ability. A surprise meeting at a hospital or working environment can lead to a romance.

Thursday the 14th. Go out with a partner to buy things needed at home. Exercise willpower so as not to overexceed your joint funds. You can find yourself feeling rather depressed and dispirited. A desire to be alone may make relations with others rather difficult.

Friday the 15th. This will not be a good day for travel. You need all documents and visas in order if you intend to go on a long journey. Careless mistakes or neglected details can make a lot of trouble for you. In-laws may prove a nuisance. If you are in legal proceedings, be prepared to have a difficult time.

Saturday the 16th. Travel is not the best thing to be doing just now, fraught as it is with delays and frustrations. It seems you have to be off somewhere on a business matter, like it or not. Meeting an important person may be your goal, but the gods seem to have decided to put as many obstacles in the way as possible.

Sunday the 17th. You will not be in the mood to stay at home. While it is fine to satisfy desires every now and then, take care not to be too impulsive in your spending. You tend to go overboard. Beautiful jewelry and clothes can look very tempting.

Monday the 18th. Take care when entering into any negotiations or agreements at work. You may need to consider certain legal angles first. However, the help of an older person or an official body of some sort may help to bring matters to completion at last. This is a day when your work is acknowledged by the public.

Tuesday the 19th. This can be an emotional day. However, you seem in a state of fine balance which helps you to cope with all that is going on around you at work and home. Surprises may be in store. A special person whom you have not seen for ages may reappear.

Wednesday the 20th. You are likely to be kept very active on the social scene. Although this can be a rather exhausting pace at times, it should all be quite enjoyable. A quarrel with a friend or a group of people has the possibility of being patched up today. There is the need for honest and good-humored exchanges.

Thursday the 21st. Although an agreement is sure to go over well with a group of people you are involved with, you need to take care that certain money issues are fully discussed first. Don't agree to just anything. A secret deal you appear to be involved in can mean meeting some very powerful and influential people.

Friday the 22nd. This can be a very good day for doing some private study or preparing for making a speech. However, you need to take care not to do too much. Your ability to express yourself may get out of hand. Why not work out what you want to say in advance?

Saturday the 23rd. The family may be able to give you some comfort and sympathy. You will need it if your health is not at its best. Some of you Libras may even have to spend some time in the hospital. Try to avoid catching chills or getting sprains. Be careful.

Sunday the 24th. A cheerful mood can transform your attitude. A new start is sure to have the effect of making you feel peaceful and balanced. If you have been ill, things are improving considerably. You may arrange to be engaged, but keep this a secret as yet.

Monday the 25th. You can convince others of your own ideas now. Your ability to put over your plans and viewpoint in a balanced, rational, yet feeling, way can be a success. If you are teaching, others can be fascinated by your words and your personality. A letter or communication you receive can inspire you.

Tuesday the 26th. This will be a restless and surprise-filled day. Nothing is likely to go according to plan, so take it all as it comes. Constant disruptions and interruptions can make you feel jumpy and uncoordinated. Family news can be sudden and upsetting.

Wednesday the 27th. Now will be the time to get down to some hard work sorting out a few money matters. Your desire to achieve more and earn more should start to produce some results now. For some of you Libras, there may be anger and animosity over petty money troubles. This can be a day for breaking things.

Thursday the 28th. For some this will be a day when you feel quite rich. You may receive a tax rebate, insurance claim, inheritance, or a boost from some unexpected source. You may find yourself clearing out the house. This can feel most therapeutic.

Friday the 29th. Traveling salespeople can find this a good day for doing business. Those in the clothing and cosmetic trade should do especially well. Your ability to be full of charm is likely to open all sorts of doors. If you are involved in study, things flow well for you.

Saturday the 30th. It can be a good idea to take things in a quiet and leisurely fashion now. Enjoy shopping about your neighborhood. Take time to write a few letters and catch up on phone calls to relatives. You may want to visit the neighbors. All in all, this will not be a time for going far afield.

Sunday October 1st. A sense of heaviness may put a damper on your personality at present. This can be due to family issues. A parental figure can be too controlling and authoritarian. Or you may find yourself acting the part of a negative parent to your children.

Monday the 2nd. Unexpected happenings at home can make this an interesting day. It will be good for organizing your resources. Deal constructively with repairs and rebuilding programs. A friend may call unexpectedly.

Tuesday the 3rd. Youngsters may figure a lot in your life. If you are a teacher, you will find them a pleasure on some trip or special seminar. This will be a good day for signing a contract or agreement.

Wednesday the 4th. Take special care with any physical activities or sports events now. Your ability to be attractive and charming these days should help you to gain the affection of another. In fact, you cannot really go wrong, as whatever you say seems to impress.

Thursday the 5th. You may have talked your way into a new contract or a new job. If you are a salesperson, this will be a good time to showcase your sales techniques. A blend of humor and fun will make what you have to say very attractive. However, attend to details.

Friday the 6th. Those of you who are caring for elderly people can find that you are able to do something positive for them now. It is a very good day for healing people and helping them in practical ways.

Saturday the 7th. This is likely to be a difficult day for personal relationships. You may find it difficult to communicate to a partner. Loved ones seem contrary. You feel excitable or nervous. You may be in the mood to raise a few eyebrows.

Sunday the 8th. Having confrontations with other people is a sure way of upsetting your sense of peace and harmony. You may have to learn a few things that may not be attractive about yourself. You may also need to strike some kind of compromise with a partner.

Monday the 9th. Things do not improve a lot in your relationship pattern. In fact, emotions may have gotten quite out of hand, especially where family matters are concerned. You may feel quite upset by unexpected reactions from parents or other family members.

Tuesday the 10th. If you had problems over money matters yesterday, you can now begin to see a new and more imaginative way of dealing with them. Use a sensitive approach to shared finances. Although things still seem muddled on the home front, your ability to be more decisive should help clear the fog.

Wednesday the 11th. It may take a bit of determination and forcefulness to get family members to see the true money situation. It may mean being more honest with your partner about your resources and possessions. This can bring about a lot of bad feeling, but it is sure to clear the air in the long run. A friend can help.

Thursday the 12th. This will be a much better day for communicating your ideas. You may need to approach a neighbor over a personal scheme or plan. Generally, it will be a good day for signing agreements. If you are a teacher, you can put things over with interest. Travel to satisfy your curiosity should be stimulating.

Friday the 13th. You are likely to encounter some delays and frustrations at work. Co-workers may seem gossipy, paranoid, or plain grumpy. An older person or an in-law may need some help and sympathy from you. Your frame of mind will be positive and peaceful.

Saturday the 14th. Trying to get associates to understand your ideas can be a real pain. Perhaps you are too emotionally involved to stand back and to state things clearly. A sibling can prove uncooperative. Let it alone; things are likely to change sooner than you expect.

Sunday the 15th. You may be called upon to run around a lot. Family members will seem lively and energetic. A warmhearted friend may call. New encounters or groups can make this a very interesting day. You enjoy stimulating money-raising activities.

Monday the 16th. If your place of work is due for a massive remodeling, you are likely to be rather ill at ease. The muddle and mess in the office are very annoying to a Libra sense of order. Repairs or alterations have to take place. Do not count the cost too much. The changes only add to the value of your business.

Tuesday the 17th. A good debate or discussion can give you a lot of intellectual pleasure now. You seem likely to be a spokesperson in this. Others are not totally in accord with your ideas. You may need to use a lot of charm and persuasion to get your way. Spending on a loved one may be more costly than you expect.

Wednesday the 18th. This will be a quiet and inactive day socially. You may feel rather bored, as matters will just tick along in a fairly routine sort of way. However, if you can use the opportunity to work out your schedules and sort out your diary, it can be useful.

Thursday the 19th. Today can be difficult, as plans go awry. You cannot keep everything under control, however hard you try. Be sure that friends do not try to manipulate you emotionally. A group can attempt to extort money from you. Just be watchful and firm; tread carefully.

Friday the 20th. After a tense and trying day, take time off to be alone for a while. Sort out your personal values and try to understand just what you truly love and respect. You may tend to feel rather alone, even rejected. It may be hard to think positively now.

Saturday the 21st. This time can be good for those who meditate or are involved in spiritual work. You may gain a sudden insight into such matters. Visiting someone in the hospital or in an institution can be a kindly act this morning. Later on, your mood will make you feel like joining in a local sports activity.

Sunday the 22nd. You are capable of covering a good deal of ground if you are busy studying. You should be alert, reasonable, and able to see life in a broad and all-embracing way. Petty matters will not interest you. Brothers and sisters play an important part.

Monday the 23rd. Your appearance or your attitude can lead others to form a wrong impression about you. It will be better to be yourself. You may fool yourself that a certain family issue is under control. Don't relax too much, as peculiar problems may come up again. Some of you may feel homesick or nostalgic.

Tuesday the 24th. At last it will seem that money matters have reached some sort of balance. An important individual may want to get together with you to make an agreement over finances. If you are able to meet early in the day, this can work out to your advantage.

Wednesday the 25th. There can be cause for celebration in your personal as well as corporate financial matters. Some of you Libra people may receive an inheritance or other surprising and possibly unexpected windfall. This can give you freedom to fulfill a few dreams. You proceed with caution and good taste.

Thursday the 26th. Lively conversations and debates make this a pleasant day. Your spirits will be high, and good humor and cheerfulness add zest to whatever is going on. Relatives are on good terms with each other and with you. You can help a neighbor or foreign visitor by being welcoming. Travel is favored.

Friday the 27th. Today is likely to be rather heavy and difficult. Your thoughts may be negative, pessimistic, and serious. Dealing with older people and their health can have a depressing effect. Co-workers can be gloomy. It will be just a mood likely soon to pass.

Saturday the 28th. This will be altogether a different day. If you are at home, you can feel quite relaxed. If you are able to go away and stay near the sea or a lake, you will feel healed and restored. It is worth a dip into joint finances to take a refreshing break.

Sunday the 29th. Do some unusual things at home. You may find that a spiritual gathering can have a profound effect on the family. Helping out with elderly people can give you both great pleasure and sense of peace. Watch what you say in case you let out some secret.

Monday the 30th. Children can pose a problem just now. Their liveliness and excitement can be hard to control. Speak to them openly and honestly. You can gain their support and encourage them to get on with study. It seems hard to make yourself clear over property negotiations. Be open and aboveboard.

Tuesday the 31st. Romantic involvements are favored now. You are in the mood. Just enjoy yourself and put cares aside for a little while. An unusual and exciting romance can begin. You may meet through a mutual family friend. If you enjoy mental games of skill and quizzes, this can be a good day for such pleasures.

Wednesday November 1st. Scenes of jealousy can make a love affair painful. If a lover is too possessive, you may feel this as a threat to your freedom and rightly so. Take care not to deceive. Secrets have a way of being found out. Later angry scenes can upset routine at home and work.

Thursday the 2nd. Health problems can make you feel slow and depressed. You feel worries and burdens weighing you down. Money matters add to this. You can upset others by a tactless and abrupt approach. Take care what you say to a friend or family member.

Friday the 3rd. A sudden change in your circumstances can perk you up and improve your health. Just working out a different daily routine can be good for some of you. For others, a new job can mean a complete and radical change of life-style. It may even mean that you will have to move your home base.

Saturday the 4th. Good spirits and cheerful conversation can make a partnership more fun. Life seems to have really picked up tempo of late. You and a mate can find yourself involved in all kinds of lively neighborhood activities, sports, or discussion groups.

Sunday the 5th. Others may try to ram spiritual ideas down your throat. Keep as detached as you can. Upsets in the family can affect a mate. A considerate attitude can do wonders in soothing precarious relationships. Partners upset you; friends can be helpful.

Monday the 6th. News of some financial deal in which you have been involved may be disappointing. It may be hard to come to any agreement with others over property and possessions. Those involved in divorce proceedings can find this a tough day for any kind of rational agreement. A car can cost a lot to repair.

Tuesday the 7th. Seeing an important person about your bank balance can be an unnerving experience. Keep cool and make sure you lay all your cards on the table. You may receive help from unexpected quarters. Those of you involved in tricky property deals need to be very watchful. Not everyone is to be trusted.

Wednesday the 8th. Some pretty intense work needs to be done to sort out a financial problem. Corporate matters will be decidedly at risk this morning. If you have to use subversive tactics to bring things back onto an even keel, then don't falter if debts are not paid.

Thursday the 9th. This will not be an easy day for traveling. Your need to rush about and get things done quickly is likely to be thwarted over foolish details. Keep as calm as you can, or you may say things impulsively that you later regret. Studies are hard to buckle down to. Legal difficulties can make life trying.

Friday the 10th. It can be hard to know where to expand and where to cut back. If you are involved in a court case, you can feel very frustrated. Officials can block every effort to clarify a situation. However, a powerful individual may be able to guide you.

Saturday the 11th. At last it may seem as if you are getting somewhere in sorting out problematic money arrangements. This will be a favorable time for those who are likely to make a public appearance or speech. Writers can see some financial rewards for their work.

Sunday the 12th. This can be the right time for making a decision and sticking to it. It may concern some spiritual matter to which you feel dedicated. Doing your duty can give you strength and self-confidence. An older person can be of importance. Your ability to deal with children will make them feel secure.

Monday the 13th. Intense involvements with a group of people can lead to some deep discussions. Many resentments may need to be aired. Concentrate on the details of what is being said, and be sure to point out your needs. Your vitality can be low.

Tuesday the 14th. You will be unusually busy with friends. Visiting museums, art galleries, and concerts in good company can be enjoyable. If you are part of a large family, gatherings with brothers and sisters can be lively. People from overseas may join in.

Wednesday the 15th. An important person may let you and your friends down over a property or money situation this morning. You are likely to feel the repercussions of this later in the day. Try not to feel too upset about it. Leading a group of people can present problems if you do not all share the same values.

Thursday the 16th. Private trading on the stock market can produce the results that can make dreams come true. Property deals are favored. You may even find the home you have always yearned for. Little shopping trips and visits to neighbors can be lively.

Friday the 17th. Attempts to seek new career training or to widen your knowledge through study can be thwarted now. You may not feel up to presenting yourself as well as usual because of a health problem. A practical and influential person can give you a lot of sympathy. Those in therapy will benefit.

Saturday the 18th. Some of you Libra people are likely to be studying new working techniques. If you are interested in repairing machinery, today should give a lot of insight into the workings of things. You can feel quite inspired. Those who love to write are sure to be more intuitive and imaginative than usual.

Sunday the 19th. You should be feeling on top of the world. Having a party or get-together with relatives and neighbors can be fun. Conversations can be inspiring. Take care not to be too sentimental, or you may be carried away with romantic illusions.

Monday the 20th. Your determination to improve your financial situation and become wealthy may bring some surprises. An influential person can pass on certain plans or make available funds for home improvements. You have a number of changes and inspirations for improving business efficiency at home and at work.

Tuesday the 21st. Taking an elderly invalid out for a shopping spree can be a very kindly act. You may need to consult an accountant about certain money matters concerning the home. If your business involves the media, this can be a good day for obtaining unusual information. Short trips should be enjoyable.

Wednesday the 22nd. Make appointments to meet with bank managers or other important individuals involved in finance. This will be a good time for any sort of financial planning. Consider how to improve efficiency and communications at work and at home. Brothers and sisters play an important role now.

Thursday the 23rd. You may be traveling to someone's house for Thanksgiving. A certain reluctance may make the journey less than pleasant. Communication over small things can become a major source of argument. Try to reach an understanding.

Friday the 24th. Today is likely to be spent in a fairly humdrum way. Taking care of the home situation will be a priority. Take advantage of the quiet time to catch up on letters, phone calls, and other neglected communications. Get things as up to date as you can.

Saturday the 25th. A great deal of useful and constructive work can be done about the home now. You are likely to be disciplined and ready to get everything organized and into some sort of shape. An elderly member of the family may need your attention.

Sunday the 26th. Unexpected happenings at home will make this a day of surprises. A friend may call and disrupt your plans. However, you will feel quite excited and ready for changes and fresh activities. Later, on an interesting trip, you may gain a lot of information that can help with research or study projects.

Monday the 27th. This is likely to be a favorable day for traveling. If your travels are for pleasure, they are also informative in an interesting way. The mind should be broadened. A good-humored approach to a romance or love affair can make a real difference.

Tuesday the 28th. The morning may see you energetically driving or walking about the local area with children. Sports activities or discussions with neighbors will be cheerful and lively. Later in the day, you may have mixed feelings about a loved one. There can be some jealousy or possessiveness on either or both sides.

Wednesday the 29th. Dealing with everyday chores and activities will keep you hard at work. You may find that you need to sort out files and other correspondence details at your workplace. It will be an opportunity for concentrated attention to finer and smaller things than usual. Some of this may bog you down a bit.

Thursday the 30th. Deal with chores and other humdrum activities at home. Dealing with family members is not easy. Their attempts to manipulate you with their ideas and demands can be frustrating. Try to keep up the spirit of compassion and detachment.

Friday December 1st. Your relationships with partners and spouses should be very good. Discussions about the education of a child can be of great importance to both of you. You may hear that an influential person needs to see you and your partner over some legal or publishing matter. A superior has good news for you.

Saturday the 2nd. Although the situation at home will be anything but clear, you will be able to discuss things with a partner in such a way that the funny side of it all can be seen. This can help sort out any confusion. You feel sentimental or regretful about the past.

Sunday the 3rd. A desire to beautify the home may keep you busy. Some Libras may begin a crash decorating program. This will be a good day for a family gathering. Warm and loving feelings seem to abound, especially with your parents. Loved ones can be caring.

Monday the 4th. If corporate and joint finances need attending to, this will be a favorable time for getting your accounts in order. Your sense of balance and discipline is likely to be at its best. Some news of a relative or neighbor may have saddened you a little.

Tuesday the 5th. Sudden changes in your joint financial arrangements can be for the better. A sudden windfall or bonus can come your way. Traveling or shopping can be upsetting. Congestion and emotional scenes make a journey unpleasant. Take care not to voice your feelings over deeply felt issues to a neighbor.

Wednesday the 6th. This is likely to be an uneasy day. If you are finishing a course of study, you may feel regret at leaving. Difficult travel can put you out. Crowds make shopping a nightmare. Try a philosophical attitude. A superior may fall out with you over your time-keeping. Children can be difficult.

Thursday the 7th. You can find it very hard to attend to details at work. Your mind appears to be full of all sorts of distracting ideas. This does not help with important discussions. It will not be a favorable day for signing any agreements or new contracts. Wait a while.

Friday the 8th. All sorts of sudden decisions and urgent matters arise and need immediate attention. Your judgment does seem wiser. A sense of humor will help keep things in perspective. Otherwise, you are sure to feel very wound up by the end of the day.

Saturday the 9th. Although you can achieve much if you are at work, it will not be easy. Upsets at home make you feel frazzled. It can be difficult to get everyone's cooperation. You may become rather hypersensitive. There will be a need to compromise and keep balance. Older people can help here.

Sunday the 10th. Have things become so bad that some of you are thinking of leaving home? Try not to let upsets and sudden disruptions get you down too much. The afternoon can see a change of mood; you seem able to soldier on and take on others' burdens.

Monday the 11th. It has been worth waiting for this day. You will enjoy a social function tonight where you will be likely to meet important, even famous, people in the writing or media world. Your own sense of calm and peacefulness makes you most attractive. A romance with an older person may come about.

Tuesday the 12th. There may not be a good deal doing on the social scene just now. However, this can give you a little space to deal with planning the week ahead. If you have a good many hopes and wishes, you can quietly sit and consider them. Make new goals for next year. Make the most of positive feelings for friends.

Wednesday the 13th. You may be feeling a bit drained emotionally. Painful experiences from the past can haunt you. Let them go if you can. You may feel as if someone is acting against you. Speaking honestly of your fears will help to clear matters up.

Thursday the 14th. You can find yourself feeling tired and sluggish now. In fact, you may be ill. Take time off if you can to relax and recuperate. A boss may not be too pleased, but you need rest. A child can become sick, and this may mean time off work.

Friday the 15th. You will be prone to say too much about a local matter. However, people in the neighborhood will be impressed by your knowledge. Work in seclusion to complete a project. Legal matters can take a sudden turn for the better.

Saturday the 16th. Family disturbances can affect you strongly. You are in a hasty, impulsive mood. This can lead to accidents in the home, so take extra care. A loved one may appear dreamy and confused. This can make you even more impatient.

Sunday the 17th. Be sure that you do not give a false impression to others about your feelings. Having an open and honest conversation with a spiritual leader may help restore confidence in your own abilities.

Monday the 18th. You take a positive interest in higher education now. Spiritual matters will mean much to you. A cheerful, generous attitude will make you popular. Firm decisions can be made about the future.

Tuesday the 19th. You are able to deal with money matters very resourcefully. Imaginative ideas flow. You can speak passionately about long-held feelings. People may react heatedly to your outbursts.

Wednesday the 20th. Surprise visitors can make this an interesting and lively day at home. Neighbors may show their appreciation by giving you unexpected gifts or food. A new friendship can lead to a romance. You can feel far more free emotionally. A spirit of adventure will make you ready to tackle anything.

Thursday the 21st. A feeling of optimism and joy can make today feel like a new beginning. Travelers or students from far away can bring joy. Important individuals may come to meet you or join your neighborhood gatherings. A renewed sense of faith is likely for those of you who belong to a spiritual group.

Friday the 22nd. This can be a great time for family gatherings. Having parties and going to open houses will be the order of the day. Those who play musical instruments may be called upon to give concerts. These will be popular and may bring fame.

Saturday the 23rd. Although you are much occupied at home, many of you will be likely to feel a spirit of detachment and peace. It will be good for those who meditate at home. Later in the day you will be very busy with social happenings and entertainment.

Sunday the 24th. You are ready to enjoy yourself and have a good time tonight. Your way of having fun will be to go out with friends who know how to be slightly unconventional. However, your communications with family members will be realistic and sensible.

Monday the 25th. Merry Christmas! Whatever your faith or belief, you can enjoy today fully. Friends and relatives will make you feel cheerful and generous. You can enjoy games and all amusements. For many, this can be quite a romantic time. It can be the day when a serious decision will be made by some Libras.

Tuesday the 26th. This can be a very peaceful day. You are sure to be glad of the chance to stick quietly to the daily routine. You can concern yourself with household chores and devise a new diet. Get yourself mentally and physically in order for the coming year.

Wednesday the 27th. Your somewhat serious and responsible frame of mind will continue. Some of you may be concerned with having put on weight. Work on new diets and regimens for healthier living. The home atmosphere will be lively and cheerful.

Thursday the 28th. An important person from the past can reappear. For some, this may mean the renewal of a romantic relationship. Others may form a valuable business partnership. It is important to make your ideas and objectives very clear to a partner.

Friday the 29th. A mate may be trying to conceal anger at your deceptions. Be open and honest about your intentions. You can be surprised at how forgiving a partner can be. Business partners need to be aboveboard in their transactions. You feel a bit discouraged by the reactions of people.

Saturday the 30th. This will be a far better day for dealing with others on a personal level. You can still be in for some surprise encounters and attitudes; however, there will be a better sense of understanding between you and loved ones. Family matters may remain tense. You don't know what to expect or how to react.

Sunday the 31st. The last day of the year will be as full of surprises as ever. You do seem to be inspired with new and intuitive ideas about how to deal with the situation at home. If joint money problems have been part of your troubles, you can work together to apply innovative methods to improving your finances.